English for
Sales &
Purchasing

EXPRESS SERIES

Lothar Gutjahr & Sean Mahoney

OXFORD
UNIVERSITY PRESS

OXFORD
UNIVERSITY PRESS

Great Clarendon Street, Oxford OX2 6DP

Oxford University Press is a department of the University of Oxford.
It furthers the University's objective of excellence in research, scholarship,
and education by publishing worldwide in

Oxford New York

Auckland Cape Town Dar es Salaam Hong Kong Karachi
Kuala Lumpur Madrid Melbourne Mexico City Nairobi
New Delhi Shanghai Taipei Toronto

With offices in

Argentina Austria Brazil Chile Czech Republic France Greece
Guatemala Hungary Italy Japan Poland Portugal Singapore
South Korea Switzerland Thailand Turkey Ukraine Vietnam

OXFORD and OXFORD ENGLISH are registered trade marks of
Oxford University Press in the UK and in certain other countries

Adapted from *English for Sales and Purchasing* by Lothar Gutjahr and
Sean Mahoney © Cornelsen Verlag GmbH & Co. OHG, Berlin 2007

The moral rights of the author have been asserted

Database right Oxford University Press (maker)

First published 2009

2013 2012 2011 2010 2009
10 9 8 7 6 5 4 3 2

ISBN: 978 0 19 457931 5

Printed in China

ACKNOWLEDGEMENTS

*The publisher would like to thank the following for their kind permission to
reproduce photographs and other copyright material*: Alamy pp 13 (trade
fair/dbimages), 46 (woman on phone/Rob Wilkinson), 57 (woman
speaker/Andrew Paterson); Getty Images p5 (businessman/Tony Garcia);
iStockphoto.com pp 5 (businesswoman/pkline), 8 (man and woman at
computer/pkline), 12 (woman, top left/texxter), (man, top right; woman,
middle left; woman, bottom right/Yuri_Arcurs), (man, bottom left/
digitalskillet), 14 (desk meeting/lisegagne), 16 (bar meeting/Thomas_
EyeDesign), 21 (businesswoman/Yuri_Arcurs), 22 (man at computer;
woman on phone/Yuri_Arcurs), 23 (wine cellar/gehringj), 24 (man on
phone/archives), (woman on phone/acilo), 26 (woman on phone/
1001nights), 28 (wineglasses/sarasang), 32 (business meeting/
monkeybusiness images), 33 (cars/Andy445), 34 (car interior/PKM1),
36 (café interior/1001nights), 37 (business meeting/RapidEye), 38
(handshake/jhorrocks), 41(hammer/Hamster3d), 42 (man on phone/
inkastudio), 44 (clothesrail/YT), 49 (woman, top left/jhorrocks), (man,
top right/shorrocks), (man, bottom left/Renphoto), (woman, bottom
right/masta4650), 55 (woman at computer/fotek), 57 (coffee sack/
migin), (half full cup/sumos), (full cup/nallevalle), (coffee beans/eAlisa),
(two people drinking coffee/nyul); webstockpro p11 (pilot and flight
attendant/CD Bank).

Artwork by: Stephen May.

Cover images courtesy of: Punchstock (main image/Rob Melnychuk/
Photodisc), (top left/Bernhard Lang/Photographer1s Choice), OUP
(bottom left/Photodisc).

Contents

About this book

English for Sales and Purchasing is for people who need to communicate effectively with international clients and colleagues. Although sales and purchasing pursue different objectives within a business, both roles require fluent business English to achieve their goals. Buyers and sales people manage international clients, deal with foreign suppliers, attend international exhibitions, draw up proposals, and deal with all manner of complaints and enquiries. **English for Sales and Purchasing** presents all the essential expressions and conversation techniques that will enable you to communicate successfully in all these situations.

The six units of **English for Sales and Purchasing** present realistic situations for sales and purchasing. The first unit provides an overview of the core activities within the purchasing and sales environment. The following units each focus on specific themes, including approaching a new client or selecting potential suppliers, the conception and development of proposals, the preparation and realization of negotiations, tying up orders and deliveries, and dealing with or making complaints.

Every unit begins with a **Starter** to introduce the topic. This is followed by dialogues, reading texts, and authentic documents as well as a variety of exercises designed to aid the learning of important vocabulary and phrases in contextual situations. In each unit you will be referred to the **Partner Files** in the back of the book. These are role-plays which enable learners to practise the vocabulary and language of the unit in realistic situations. The units end with **Output** activities, which consist of reading texts to extend the unit topic or offer further useful tips, and they also provide opportunities for discussion. When you have finished all the units, you can **Test yourself!** with a fun crossword at the back of the book.

At the back of **English for Sales and Purchasing** there is an **Answer key** so that you can check your answers independently. There is also an **A–Z word list** and a **Useful phrases** list that you can refer to when preparing to speak to customers and colleagues. You will also find phrases in this section that you can use to make small talk on a variety of topics.

The **MultiROM** contains all the **Listening extracts** from the book. These can be played through the audio player on your computer, or through a conventional CD-player. In order to give yourself extra listening practice, listen to it in your car or download it to your MP3-player and listen when you are out and about. The **Interactive exercises** let you review by doing exercises that cover the essential language from the book on your computer; this will be particularly valuable if you are using the book for self-study.

Jobs and responsibilities

Look at the following tasks. Which do you do in your job? Which do you do in English? Compare your answers with a partner's.

	often	sometimes	never	English
make phone calls				
write emails				
fill in forms				
do Internet searches				
go on business trips				
take part in meetings				
take clients out for meals				
give presentations				
do market research				
go to trade fairs				
handle customer complaints				

Which of the tasks above are typical for people working in sales? Which are typical for people working in purchasing? Discuss with a partner.

AUDIO

2–3

1 **Carol Sayers and Kim Dong-Sun both work for Interflights, an air carrier located near Seoul. Listen to them describe their jobs. Who works in sales and who works in purchasing?**

Listen again and decide who does the following as part of his/her job.

	Carol	Dong-Sun
1 calls and visits clients		
2 writes emails		
3 collects and compares offers		
4 presents products		
5 liaises with other departments		
6 does market research		
7 makes offers		
8 negotiates contracts		
9 goes to trade fairs		
10 deals with tenders		
11 handles complaints		
12 writes reports		

2 Match the two parts to make phrases used by Carol and Dong-Sun.

a	to negotiate	date
b	to handle	tenders
c	market	order forms
d	to fill in	contracts
e	delivery	complaints
f	to draw up	research

Now match the phrases a–f to the definitions 1–6.

1 To write down the information needed to purchase goods or services. `d`

2 Collecting information about what customers buy, and why.

3 To write a formal request to suppliers asking them to present their proposals or offers.

4 To try to reach an agreement about details like price, quantity, discounts, etc.

5 The goods have to be delivered by this time.

6 To take care of customers' problems.

Match the job ads from a British newspaper on the next page to the job titles below.

key account manager ☐   senior purchaser ☐

sales representative ☐   supply chain manager ☐

1

The ideal candidate will be responsible for the ordering and sales of the products as well as the identification of new business opportunities. He/She will be required to be flexible and will be able to offer excellent customer service.

3

This is a senior sales role with a strong focus on improving key and strategic accounts. As a senior member of the team, you will be responsible for managing specific global, multinational and national retailers as well as identifying and exploiting new business opportunities.

2

This will be a key position within the production and commercial operations. Reporting to the Production Director, the main responsibility of this position is to manage, control and record the flow of products from our own and third party production sites.

4

The key skills requirements are as follows:

- A proven record in negotiations and cost savings
- Knowledge of materials used in the manufacture of furniture
- Ability to create and develop supplier relationships
- Skills in sourcing products and services
- Ability to work within a project team environment

4   Match the following job titles with the descriptions below.

1   key account manager ☐

2   senior purchaser (or buyer) ☐

3   sales representative ☐

4   supply chain manager ☐

5   strategic buyer ☐

6   regional sales manager ☐

7   sourcing (or procurement) officer ☐

8   customer service manager ☐

a   makes sure that clients' needs are met and helps customers when things go wrong

b   is responsible for specific sales accounts and direct client contact

c   is responsible for strategic planning (i.e. making sure a company has everything necessary for production, including machines and new production sites)

d   negotiates with suppliers about long-term or frame contracts

e   is in charge of making and maintaining contact with clients within a specific geographical area

f   is responsible for large clients, especially for clients of strategic interest to the company

g   is in charge of a team of purchasers

h   is in charge of logistics and of making sure suppliers meet demands

What is your job title? How would you describe what you do in English?

JOB TITLES

Job titles in most countries are usually determined by the person's position in the hierarchy, their payment, and whether they are legally allowed to represent their company and sign contracts, for example. This is not always the case in the U.S., the U.K. and other English-speaking countries. The job titles there often give you no clear indication of the person's responsibilities because each company has a different structure and operates under different rules. Thus a vice president (V.P.) in one organization may have a very different job description from a V.P. in another company.

5 You are taking part in a seminar with people from other companies. Use language from the box to prepare a short presentation on your company, the department you work in and, especially, your job and responsibilities. Then give the presentation to a partner or the group.

> **TALKING ABOUT YOUR JOB**
>
> **Describing the company/department**
> I work in the sales/purchasing
>   department of a small/medium-sized/
>   large company called ...
> We develop/make/produce/sell/...
> Our department is divided into ...
> We need to liaise/work closely with ...
> We also are more actively involved in ...
> My team/group makes sure that ...
>
> **Describing responsibilities**
> My team is responsible for ...
> I am in charge of ...
> My main responsibility is ...
> A lot of our/my work involves ...
> We have to/need to ...
> I spend a lot of time ...
> My job also includes ...

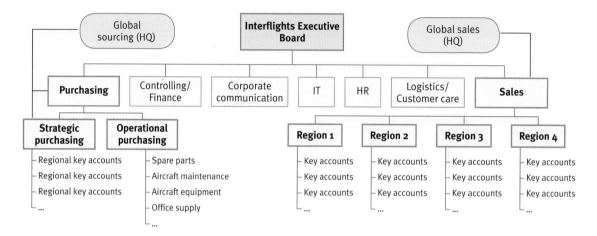

6 A fellow member of the sales department at Interflights is filling Carol Sayers in on a meeting she missed. Listen and decide which topics from the agenda they discuss.

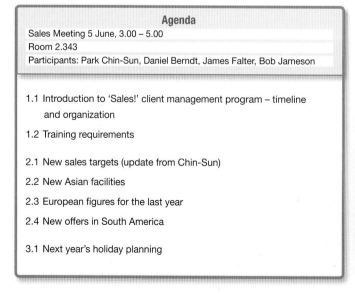

Listen again to the dialogue. Complete these sentences.

1   ... first of all, Chin-Sun has revised our _____.

2   She wants to _____ by ten per cent overall.

3   There are also some _____ for the various regions.

4   It certainly means we will be _____ our new targets, if it all works out.

5   Did Chin-Sun present my ideas for _____ there?

6   We will also need a _____ specifically for the region.

7   I'll _____ that, although I'm afraid it might _____.

8   I could also contact the _____ in my area.

TALKING ABOUT GOALS, OBJECTIVES AND TARGETS

The words *goal*, *objective,* and *target* have similar meanings. *Goals* tend to be long-term and are often used to refer to company plans, for example. The word *objectives* is often used in more formal situations to refer to specific things people want to achieve (objectives of a meeting, for example). In both sales and purchasing, however, or whenever money or figures are involved, the most frequently used word is *target*. Here are some expressions with *target*:

to set a target	*to be above/below target*
to be on target	*to exceed a target*
to reach a target	*to revise a target*

---

7 **Complete the sentences with the correct form of the expressions from the box.**

1   Management should be satisfied. We _____ right _____ target this year.

2   Unfortunately, last year we _____ well _____ target, so we had to cut the number of our sales team.

3   The board of directors _____ already _____ our new sales targets for next year.

4   After the stock market crash last year, we had to _____ our targets.

5   This year has gone very well for us and the way it looks now, we should _____ our targets by at least fifteen per cent.

6   We had a couple of big orders, which enabled us to _____ the target by the end of the third quarter. Hopefully, it will continue like this.

7   We _____ easily _____ our profitability targets. HQ will be happy to hear that, I'm sure.

8 Look at these expressions with the word *sales*.

Match the expressions above with the definitions below.

1 The amount of goods sold by a company.
2 The complete team of people working in sales.
3 An amount which must be paid to the government for every item sold.
4 The level of sales that a sales team wants to reach.
5 An occasion where the members of a sales team get together to discuss results and make plans.
6 The amount which has been sold of a product.
7 A set of activities designed to increase the sales of a product.
8 A man or woman working in the sales department.

AUDIO

5

9 Kim Dong-Sun from Interflights is making a telephone call to his colleague John, one of the flight crew coordinators. Listen and complete the two gaps in the requisition form.

REQUISITION FORM	Req no TR12983S-0701
Description of goods/services:	_____ _____ 1
Click here to enter details	
Date goods/services required:	*1 July*
Person making the request:	_____ 2
Date:	*20 March*
Click here to enter quotes	

Listen again and tick ✔ the correct statements. Are the kinds of suggestions Dong-Sun makes typical of purchasers at your company? Why, or why not?

1 John is interested in getting company credit cards for the flight crew. ☐

2 The flight crew often need to get cash when away on business. ☐

3 There are no suppliers on the market for the credit cards Dong-Sun has requested. ☐

4 Dong-Sun suggests some solutions that John had not thought of. ☐

5 John will make an assessment of the various offers and compare them. ☐

6 John is unhappy because Dong-Sun is taking too much time to find a solution. ☐

10 **Complete the table with verbs and nouns from the unit so far.**

VERB	NOUN
to agree	1
to assess	2
3	comparison
to compete	4
to complain	5
to purchase	6
to request	7
8	solution
to specify	9
to supply	10

6

11 **John is informing his department about the credit card issue discussed in exercise 9. Complete this excerpt with the correct form of words from the table above. Then listen to check your answers.**

So I wanted to update you all on the situation with the various offers purchasing has received for credit cards for the international flight crew. Dong-Sun's team is currently _____ ¹ these offers. The _____ ² is very tough at the moment, which is of course good for us. Not all _____ ³ were able to meet our _____ ⁴, so they were able to exclude some offers straight away. They will have to _____ ⁵ the rest very carefully and perhaps put in some _____ ⁶ for more information. But the people in our purchasing department are very thorough, and I'm sure that they will find the best _____ ⁷ for us.

TELEPHONE LANGUAGE

Saying who you are	**Getting through to the right person**
This is Adam Bedser from XYZ Ltd.	Could/Can I speak to John Murphy, please?
It's David Jones from purchasing.	I'd like to speak to somebody in your sales/
Hi Sarah. It's Frank here.	purchasing department, please.
	Is Michelle there at the moment?

---

12   **Work with a partner. Use the information in the Partner Files to practise a telephone dialogue between someone in purchasing (Partner A) and someone in sales (Partner B). Look at the phrases above before starting.**

PARTNER FILES ➤ Partner A   File 1, p. 60
Partner B   File 1, p. 62

OUTPUT   **Read these comments that people in sales and purchasing departments have given about working together. Which do you agree with?**

Veronica Lu, Head of Sales
When we had to streamline our processes last year, we salespeople had a terrible time with our purchasers. It always takes them too long to do their 'shopping', and therefore it takes our company too long to produce our goods. It really is a disaster!

Marcel Le Maigre, Account Manager
Cooperation between buyers and salespeople within one company? Never heard of it. Whatever would they need to talk to each other about?

Emma Wild, Sales Representative
Buyers buy. And sales reps sell. So buyers and sellers are 'natural enemies'; they are on opposite sides, have opposing interests and quite a different mentality. Of course they deal with each other in separate companies, but in the same company? No. How could they possibly cooperate?

Maria Santos, Senior Purchaser
Sales and purchasing are all part of producing and delivering goods or services to a customer. If the two departments don't cooperate well in the process, the company will lose money. It's as simple as that.

Edward McCoy, Managing Director
In our company, the people in the sales and purchasing departments are experts in various markets and they all try to stay on top of developments. They negotiate about quality, delivery time and, most importantly, about prices. In our company, we learn from each other through regular meetings. It works.

OVER TO YOU

- Describe the cooperation between the sales and purchasing departments in your company.
- How often do you liaise with people in other departments? Which departments do you deal with?
- What could be the benefits of close cooperation between purchasing, sales, production, and other departments in a company?

2 New contacts

STARTER

The sentences below were overheard at a trade fair. Work with a partner to decide whether the speakers work in purchasing or sales. Write **P** or **S** (or both) in the box.

a Could you tell us about the payment options? ☐

b Would you please give me some background about your company? ☐

c You'll find all our brochures on the table over there. ☐

d How much does this cost if we order 500? ☐

e Are there any other questions we need to talk about? ☐

f Would you need any additional features? ☐

g Does your sub-contractor also have a stand here? ☐

h When could we arrange a presentation of our products for you? ☐

i What guarantees do you provide? ☐

j Let me give you my card. ☐

Now discuss these questions with your partner.

1 What is your experience of trade fairs?
2 Do you think trade fairs are good for business? Why, or why not?
3 What other possibilities are there for establishing new contacts or finding new products?

1 **Donald Adams, a sales rep at Aircraft Maintenance Inc. in Liverpool, has just finished a presentation of his company's products at *The Maintenance, Repair and Overhaul (MRO) Services and Products* trade fair in Brussels. Listen to this conversation with a potential customer, Brigitte Dupont of Air South, Brussels, and say whether the following sentences are true ✔ or false ✘ .**

1 Donald has met Brigitte before. ☐

2 Brigitte thinks that Donald's company has some interesting products. ☐

3 Donald will call Brigitte after the fair is over. ☐

2 **Listen again to the conversation. Complete the sentences for how:**

1   Brigitte introduces herself.

_____ . *Brigitte Dupont.* _____ .

2   Brigitte says that the presentation was important for her.

Well, I found it very _____ *. ... yours was definitely* _____ .

3   Donald asks about Brigitte's job.

Can I ask _____ ?

4   Brigitte says what her job is.

I'm _____ .

5   Donald asks Brigitte about her interest in his company.

Do you think that our MRO services _____ ?

6   Donald asks about setting up a meeting.

Well, if you have time next week, _____ .

7   Donald asks for Brigitte's business card.

_____ *your card?*

8   Donald offers Brigitte a catalogue.

In the meantime, _____ ?

BEING POLITE

Generally, the less direct you say something in English, the more polite it sounds. Using the structures and language below will make you appear friendlier, especially to native speakers of English.

Asking indirect questions

What company are you with? → **Can I ask** *which company you are with?*

Give me your card. → **Could you** *give me your card?*

You have an office here, right? → **Doesn't your company** *have an office here?*

Using would/could

Look at our new catalogue. → **Would you like to** *look at our new catalogue?*

I will come to your office next week. → **I could** *come to your office next week.*

Are you interested in meeting after the fair? → **Would you be** *interested in meeting after the fair?*

---

3 **Make the following sentences more polite.**

1   What's your name?
2   What business are you in?
3   I want to meet you next week.
4   Wait until I get my diary.
5   Give me your contact information.
6   You work at HT Electronics, right?
7   Do you want to meet later to discuss the details?
8   Put your name on our mailing list.

4 **Match the sentences on the left with the responses on the right.**

1 Could we meet next week? Say, Wednesday?

2 I'll send you those details. When do you need them exactly?

3 Would you mind giving me your business card?

4 Could we meet after the fair to discuss this in more detail?

5 I'll prepare our offer and email it to you by next Friday.

6 I'll talk to the head of my department and ring you tomorrow.

a No, not at all. Here it is.

b Yes, good idea. When could you come to my office?

c Yes, of course. That's fine. How about 11.00?

d OK, but I'm only in the office in the morning. Can you call before noon?

e I really need them by Tuesday if possible.

f That's great. I look forward to getting it.

ESTABLISHING CONTACT AT A TRADE FAIR

Greetings and introductions
Good morning/afternoon.
Hello. My name is …
Please call me …
May/Can I introduce myself?
Nice/Pleased to meet you (too).

Moving on to business
How did you like the presentation?
What do you think of …?
Have you found anything of interest?
What line of business are you in?
Let me give you/Here's my (business) card.

Arranging to follow-up
Would it be possible to set up/arrange/fix a meeting?
Could I call you in the next few days/come to see you?
Perhaps I could send you some information.
Would you be interested in meeting after the fair is over?
Could you send me your price lists?
I'll send you an email/give you a call next week.

---

5 **Work with a partner to practise meeting someone at a trade fair for the first time. First look at the phrases above, then follow the flow chart or make a dialogue to fit your own situation.**

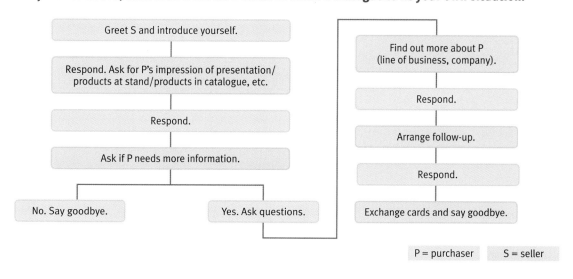

AUDIO
🔊
8

6 Two businessmen are having lunch in a pub at the annual trade fair *MRO Services and Products* in Brussels. Listen to this excerpt from their conversation and tick ✔ the topics they talk about.

Brussels ☐   beer ☐   the weather ☐

politics ☐   sports ☐   intercultural differences ☐

work ☐   music ☐   their accommodation ☐

Listen again and tick the sentences you hear.

1   a   It reminds me very much of England.
    b   It makes me think of England.
2   a   It's certainly an interesting place to have a fair.
    b   I think it's a nice place to have a fair, don't you?
3   a   Do you like football?
    b   Are you interested in football?
4   a   I see trade fairs as a place to get to know people …
    b   For me, trade fairs are more about getting to know people …
5   a   May I ask if you already have some information about my company?
    b   Let me tell you a bit about my company.
6   a   Now, let me buy you another beer.
    b   Now, tell me, what's your favourite Belgian beer?

SMALL TALK

In many parts of the world, small talk is an essential part of business. It is seen as an important 'tool' to get to know your business partner and to establish rapport, which can be the key to a good business relationship. Here are some ways to start a conversation:

> *Is this your first time here/in Belgium?*
> *What do you think of Brussels/the fair?*
> *Are you interested in football/films/winter sports?*
> *The weather here has just been fantastic/horrible.*

You can keep the conversation going by asking a follow-up question of your own. Also, instead of just answering questions with *yes* or *no*, giving detailed answers can often lead to other questions and comments.

> *Are you interested in any particular sport?*
> *– Yes, I'm really into snowboarding. How about you?*
>
> *Have you been to Liverpool?*
> *– Yes, I've been there many times. I really like the atmosphere, and the people are friendly.*

When you are ready to move on to business, you can use a sentence starting with *so* or *right* to signal the change of subject.

> *So, you are looking for suppliers?*
> *Right, shall we get down to business?*

7 Put the words in the right order to make small-talk questions, and then match them to the responses (a–f).

1 What think fair trade so you far the do of ? ☐
2 you Have to been Wimbledon ever ? ☐
3 stay Are to whole you the planning week ? ☐
4 Chicago the at weather in the is moment How ? ☐
5 Do in countries fairs are different you think other ? ☐
6 Brussels you look to a chance Have had around ? ☐

a Unfortunately not. I have to leave on Wednesday.
b Yes, I've been twice now. I love the atmosphere there, and I'm a big tennis fan.
c Not much better than here actually. Maybe a little colder, so I'm happy to be away.
d I'm really enjoying it. But I'm afraid I'll only be able to see half the stands before I leave tomorrow!
e Not yet, unfortunately. I'm hoping to have some time after the fair is over.
f Well, I think maybe the stands in England are a little more entertaining.

How can the speakers keep the conversation going? Match these follow-up questions with the exchanges above.

A And what's the weather like in Madrid now? ☐
B What about you? How long are you staying? ☐
C Have you ever been to a trade fair in England? ☐
D Oh, you're leaving so soon. Where are you off to? ☐
E What about you? Are you interested in any particular sport? ☐
F You know Brussels well. Can you recommend some things for me to see? ☐

8 Look at these small-talk questions and think of responses to keep the conversation going.

1 Isn't London great for going to the theatre?

2 Do you like this style of architecture?

3 Do you visit trade fairs all over Europe?

4 Have you ever been skiing in America?

9 Discuss these questions about small talk with a partner.

1 Do you know any other small-talk phrases? Which ones do you find most useful to get conversations going in a business context?
2 What small-talk questions do you usually ask on the telephone? How are they different from the ones you ask face-to-face?
3 Have you been in a situation where you had to make small talk with a native speaker of English? What was easy or difficult? Share your experiences with the group.

10 Look at the checklist below to help you prepare for a conversation at the *www.business.org* trade fair. Work with a partner. Use the information in your Partner File to do the role-play.

1 Remember to greet your partner, including exchanging names.

2 Use small talk to warm up a little.

3 Move on to business. You could ask for information on what your partner does.

4 What else do you need to know about your potential partner?

5 Be prepared at some stage to answer questions about yourself and about your company.

6 Arrange the next contact/meeting.

7 Say goodbye.

PARTNER FILES Partner A File 2, p. 60
Partner B File 2, p. 62

11 After meeting again at the trade fair, Brendan from Aircraft Maintenance Inc. and Rainer from Low Cost Flights International are now back at their offices and need to exchange some information. Complete the email with words from the box.

additional • appreciated • arrange • attached • kind • like • pleasure • suggest

From: Brendan Johnson (brendan.johnson@aircraftmaintenance.co.uk) To: Rainer Noack (r.noack@lcfi.de)

Subject: Additional information about our products and services   Attachment: products.pdf

Dear Rainer,

It was a _____[1] meeting you last week at the pub in Brussels and I very much

_____[2] our conversation at your stand.

You will find the _____[3] information about our products and services that you

requested _____[4] to this email, as promised.

I would very much _____[5] to visit you soon and present our special package offer

for VIP aircrafts. Could I _____[6] a meeting at your premises in Bremen?

Please let me know if we could _____[7] a meeting and if you need any additional

information.

_____[8] regards,

Brendan

EMAILS

There are fewer conventions with emails than with letters, but here are a few points to remember.

Opening sentence
This should always start with a capital letter. The first sentence is usually a bit of small talk, refers to a previous message or meeting, or explains why you are writing.
> *Hope you had a nice weekend./How are things going?*
> *It was nice to meet you at the conference last week.*
> *I'm writing to tell/ask you about .../I just wanted to get in touch to ...*

Salutations and closes
Although there are no rules about which salutation or close to use, here are some guidelines:

more formal	*Dear Mr, Mrs, Ms*	*Regards/Sincerely*
	Dear Bob	*Best wishes/Kind regards*
	Hello/Hi Bob	*All the best/Best*
least formal	*(no salutation*)*	*(just first name or initials*)*

(* usually just with colleagues and especially during long email exchanges)

---

12 **Brendan and Rainer have exchanged emails to arrange to meet, but the paragraphs have been mixed up. Sort the paragraphs a–g into the correct emails below.**

a Thank you very much for the invitation and the opportunity to meet. I would like to confirm the meeting for 3 April at 11 a.m. Let me suggest that I bring our specialist who could add more details both to the presentation and the discussion afterwards.

b Would 3 April at 11 a.m. at our offices be convenient for you?

c We would be very happy to invite you to our office in Bremen, and would be interested in a presentation for four of us (my boss, two colleagues of mine, and myself). I suggest about an hour and a half, with lunch to follow.

d I look forward to seeing you in Bremen.

e Thank you for your help. Looking forward to seeing you on 3 April.

f I would also like to take the opportunity to find out more about your specific needs and wishes. Would you mind answering the following questions to help us with our preparation?
  • What number of aircraft are you interested in?
  • At which locations will you require these services?
  • Will you also be interested in regular overhauls?

g It was good to meet you and I also enjoyed your visit to our stand. Thank you also for the file you sent with your recent email; it was exactly the information I needed. We would like to hear more about your MRO services for VIP aircrafts specifically.

From: Rainer Noack
To: Brendan Johnson
Subject: Re: Additional information about our products and services

Dear Brendan,

1 ☐

2 ☐

3 ☐

4 ☐

Best wishes,
Rainer

From: Brendan Johnson
To: Rainer Noack
Subject: Our presentation

Dear Rainer,

5 ☐

6 ☐

7 ☐

Kind regards,
Brendan

13 **Now find phrases in the two emails on page 19 to complete the gaps below.**

Introduction/Referring to previous meeting or message
Regarding our conversation of 3 January, ...

_____ 1

_____ 2

Requesting information
Could you send me some details about ...

_____ 3

_____ 4

Making or confirming an appointment
How about Thursday at 4 p.m?

_____ 5

_____ 6

Concluding
Please feel free to contact me again.

_____ 7

_____ 8

14 **Use Rainer's and Brendan's notes to write emails to other people they met at the trade fair. Try to use phrases from this unit.**

Brendan

1 Email to Maria Santos from Euroflights. Good to meet her at the trade fair. Catalogue is on its way. Is weather better now?

2 Email to Kerstin Mueller. What did she think of the trade fair? I'll be in the Graz area soon. Can we arrange a meeting? Say 2 hours on 5 or 6 September?

Rainer

1 Email to Youla Kostalas at Island Jets. Will she be in northern Germany next week, like she said? Can she come to present her products, maybe Thursday afternoon?

2 Email to Michael O'Brian. Very good stand. Please send brochure and price lists. Will he ever be in Bremen? We could visit the Irish pub.

Marijke Veenstra is Head of Sales at IT International, a company based in the Netherlands. She has given an interview for the company's in-house magazine. Do you agree with the tips she gives?

INTERVIEW   9

Q: Marijke, you have been in sales for a long time, if I may say so. What are your tips for people just starting out?

A: I have four tips. First of all, the focus for any successful salesperson is building relationships with clients. If I can relate to them as people – and not just as clients – I have a better understanding of how they think, what is important for them and how they like to make their decisions. Small talk is an important tool for doing this. I ask my clients what they do on vacation, what kind of hobbies they have and I try to remember their birthdays or other details that are important to them.

This is directly linked to my second point: I have to be seen to be at my clients' side, to be able to solve their problems with my products and services. I need to think from their perspective, their market. In that way I can offer them not only a product, but a benefit – hopefully the exact benefit they are looking for. The main task of a salesperson is to 'buy' time from your client in order to find out about the benefit or benefits they expect. Often that requires asking the right questions.

The third strategic question is: how can I recognize that I have 'made an impact'? Here I need to watch my counterpart's reactions – what they say, what their body language says and sometimes even what they do not say. There is always a moment when the buyers make the mental decision to buy. Of course they don't say this out loud. But there are lots of subtle hints, like when a client says 'we' for the first time or when he talks about the future. Once I know that the client has said 'yes', I need to make fewer concessions. Again, it is the same principle really: understand your clients' needs, interests and the benefit they are seeking.

Finally, I would expect any successful salesperson to look for a 'point of contact' or an internal ally in the client organization. That should be a person who will think of 'me' when the company needs a solution, a person who prefers to work with me, rather than my competitors. The basis for that kind of contact is trust. Trust in the quality of services and goods, trust in our offers and promises. Clients compare what they expect with what they get. Trust increases when that comparison is positive. And that is positive for us! ■

IT INTERNATIONAL

OVER TO YOU

- How many 'personal things' do you know about your clients or the suppliers you work with? What 'small-talk' questions do you normally ask/do they normally ask you? Which questions are most effective for establishing a good working relationship?
- How do you think you can find a firm 'point of contact' in your clients' organization?
- What are your tips for being successful in your line of work?

3 Offers

STARTER **Look at these comments made by people in sales and purchasing about dealing with offers. Which sentences can you most identify with? Discuss with a partner.**

Sales   **Purchasing**

I have learned not to offer a price tag too early because when the other side then offers their price, I would have to meet in the middle – their 'middle'.

I wish salespeople would listen to my needs before trying to convince me of their products.

It seems from some of the offers we get that they haven't even read our specifications.

Before sending an offer, I make sure that I have talked to the person in charge of approving it.

Some tenders are so vague, we don't know what product we should offer.

Sometimes I receive offers although I don't even need the product.

The most important thing is to make it clear when writing up the offer that the customer can't do without our product.

We often have to postpone sending out invitations to tender because of last-minute changes requested by other departments in the company.

Now discuss these questions with your partner.

1   What are the procedures for dealing with offers in your company? How much of your sales or purchasing is done through open or invited tenders?
2   What sort of problems have you had when dealing with offers?
3   How often do you make or receive offers in English? Are there any differences in terms of content or format from those in your language?

OFFERS, TENDERS, AND BIDS

Offer is the general term used to describe what the salesperson is willing to give, and at what price.

Salesperson	*We have sent our offer in the post.*
Purchaser	*We have received four offers from different suppliers.*

The terms *tender* and *bid* can often be used interchangeably. Purchasers send out *an invitation to tender* (often shortened to *a tender*) when they want to receive offers from different suppliers. This can also be called *a request for proposal*. Salespeople file or submit a tender, often in competition with other suppliers, when they make their formal written offer to supply goods or services at a specific price and under specific conditions.

Salesperson	*We have **sent in** our tender/bid.*
Salesperson	*We have been **invited to** tender/bid.*
Purchaser	*We should **make a call for** tenders/bids for this product.*
Purchaser	*We have already **put out** a tender/bid for this product.*
Purchaser	*We would like to **invite you to make** a tender/bid.*

1 **Match the two parts to make sentences about offers, tenders, and bids.**

1 Have we received
2 We have already put out a
3 Before we draw up the invitation to bid,
4 The deadline for filing
5 One of our clients is interested in the new product range and
6 We put the job out
7 When will they let us know if

a our bid has been accepted?
b for tender a week ago.
c ABC Supply's offer yet?
d tenders is 30 March.
e we need to talk to the project manager again.
f has asked us to make an offer.
g tender for this project.

AUDIO

9

2 **Marco Falcone is a sales rep for Vino Rubinetto, a wine distributor located in Milan. He is calling one of his regular customers, Ines Stoll, a purchaser at Clever Catering in Copenhagen, to tell her about a new product. Listen and answer these questions.**

a What new product is Marco trying to sell?
b How does Ines indicate that she may be interested in a possible offer from Marco?
c What will happen after the phone call?

Listen again to the dialogue and complete these sentences.

1 Well, this month we _____
some of our new products in Europe, and we thought

Clever Catering _____ .

2 We're always interested _____
what's new.

3 ... we _____ of the quality
of our products, of course, but it's quite nice to receive

_____ .

4 Yes, I saw it mentioned _____

and I read something _____ .

5 Do you think this wine _____ to you and your clients?

6 ... I can tell you now that we are _____ you special rates for your first order ...

7 And I'm sure _____ with this wine, Ines.

3   Match the two parts to make phrases.

1 to put out   a quality
2 to promote   b of interest
3 special   c a tender
4 to be   d our new product
5 to place   e an order
6 high   f rates

Now use the phrases to complete the sentences below.

1 As you have been a client of ours for a long time, we are
able to offer you _____
for the first twelve months.

2 We will be looking _____ , as we need to increase sales.

3 It is our policy to accept only _____ products.

4 We are hoping this new product of ours will _____ to you.

5 Our production department has installed the necessary equipment, and we will therefore be ready

_____ next week.

6 This will be our largest purchase of the year, and we need to compare as many offers as possible,

so we think we should _____ .

4   Read this excerpt from an article in the *Successful Selling* magazine. How effective do you think this approach to selling is (from both the seller's and the buyer's point of view)?

A I D A

When salespeople think about a client's reaction to their offers, they often think of these four steps:

A for Attention
They first try to attract their client's **attention** to their products or services. Here first impressions count so it's important to be natural, honest, and professional.

I for Interest
They then try to spark the client's **interest** so that he/she wants to find out more about the product or service. The seller needs to convince the client of the advantages of the product or service and its relevance to him/her.

D for Desire
If the client has understood the benefits, and also trusts the seller, he/she will start to develop **desire** for the product or service.

A for Action
Desire results in **action**, meaning the client makes the decision to find out more or buy. ■

AUDIO
9

Now listen again to the dialogue in exercise 2 (or look at the transcript on page 71). Do you think Marco followed this approach? Why, or why not?

5   Here are some typical sentences from conversations about offers. First, decide who says each of the phrases and write **S** for seller or **P** for purchaser in the box.

1 I think you'll find that our product meets your specifications precisely. *S*
2 Interesting. Could you give me some background information? ☐
3 This month we are promoting some of our new products and we thought you might be interested. ☐
4 You'll be pleased to hear that our after-sales package is the best in the industry. ☐
5 Perhaps you would be interested in looking at our new product. ☐
6 So, I've got the go-ahead from my boss and we'd like to place the order … ☐
7 Great, sounds interesting. Can you send us an estimate for the project? ☐
8 Once you've examined the sample, I'm sure you'll be impressed with the quality and design. ☐
9 That might be exactly what we are looking for. ☐
10 OK, I'll send you an offer and we can take it from there. ☐

Now decide which of the sentences above can be used to:

a get somebody's ATTENTION? _____
b spark INTEREST in or DESIRE for the product? *1,* ___

c express INTEREST in or DESIRE for a product? _____
d show ACTION, i.e. show that the sale could take place? _____

6 Work with a partner to practise a phone call. First agree on a product and write some notes (seller) or questions to ask (purchaser). Then follow the flow chart below.

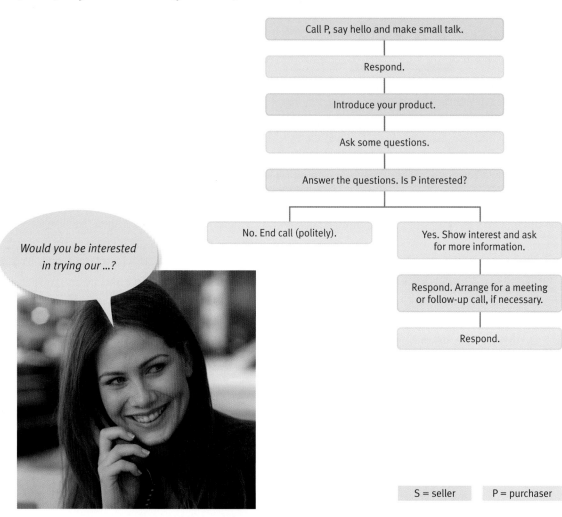

> Call P, say hello and make small talk.
>
> Respond.
>
> Introduce your product.
>
> Ask some questions.
>
> Answer the questions. Is P interested?

> No. End call (politely).

> Yes. Show interest and ask for more information.
>
> Respond. Arrange for a meeting or follow-up call, if necessary.
>
> Respond.

Would you be interested in trying our ...?

S = seller   P = purchaser

TALKING ABOUT A PRODUCT

Asking if your partner is interested
Would you be interested in trying our ...?
Perhaps I can tempt you to sample our ...?
Do you think your company might be interested in ...?
Do you think this may be of interest to you and your clients?

Showing interest
That sounds interesting.
That would certainly be of interest to us.
That might be exactly what we are looking for.
Could you send me a sample/give me some more information?

Being cautious
Well, maybe. But I would need to know more about ...
I'm not so sure.
I don't think that's really what we're looking for.
That (really) depends on your conditions/price.

Saying you are not interested
I'm sorry but ...
Unfortunately we're not looking for that at the moment.
Thanks, but we already have a supplier for that product.
No, thanks. We're not interested in that at this stage.

7 **Ines Stoll from Clever Catering has drawn up a Request for Proposal (RFP) for Vino Rubinetto. Use the words below to complete the gaps in the form.**

Bidding • Budget • Delivery • Service • Shipping • Specification • Warranty

Request for Proposal (No. 1238 HG)

Description of Product or _____ [1] (mandatory information)	
Purchaser:	*Ines Stoll, Copenhagen*
_____ [2] period (until …):	*15 October*
_____ [3] number: (consecutive numbering for each client designated by the purchaser, including the year of placing the tender)	*SEC-D 90451/010*
Category of product or service:	*Sparkling red wine, Prosecco*
Client/User:	*Sales (Clever Catering; Denmark, Germany, Britain, Belgium, Netherlands)*
Bidder/Contractor (incl. contact):	*Vino Rubinetto, Milan, Italy*
Specification of Product or Service (mandatory information)	
Kind of product or service:	*Sparkling red wine, dry, low alcohol, produced in 2006 Prosecco, medium dry produced in 2009*
Specification of performance level:	*EU Quality Standards level 1*
_____ [4] specifications:	*Sparkling red wine: €25.50 per bottle Prosecco (medium dry): €24.00 per bottle*
_____ [5] and other performances (time, conditions, terms of payment, etc.):	*Each category in 3–5 batches to warehouses in Germany, Britain, Belgium, Netherlands between March and May*
General Conditions (please fill in if relevant)	
Necessary information in advance:	
Provision of materials by the client:	*Standard bottle, 750 ml, glass, clear*
Required qualifications of the contractor:	*Own production, experience in EU markets*
Technical provisions (software/hardware/materials):	
_____ [6]:	*Replacement of all damaged goods*
After-sales services:	*Product available for minimum of 10 years*
Other information (please fill in if relevant)	

_____ [7] costs are to be included in the offer and need to be on a fixed-price basis.

_____
Date

_____
Signature (contractor confirming the offer)

Information about this tender
This document does not constitute an order nor does it create any liabilities on the part of Clever Catering.

THE TENDERING (OR BIDDING) PROCESS

The standard tendering processes are quite similar in most countries. They can consist of *invited tenders*, where only a few vendors are asked to submit bids, or *open tenders*, where a large number of companies may participate without pre-screening. Sometimes the contents of a tender can even be partly negotiated. Whether a company calls for tenders or not depends largely on the industry, the company policy, and the kind of goods or services purchasers are looking for.

8 **Match these words and phrases found in the RFP with their definitions.**

1   required qualifications ☐

2   performance level ☐

3   batch ☐

4   provision ☐

5   specifications ☐

6   fixed-price basis ☐

7   warranty ☐

a   supply
b   when a particular price is agreed and cannot be changed
c   a written agreement to repair or replace something if there is a problem
d   the exact details of a product
e   a description of how high the quality must be
f   a number of things (e.g. goods) that are dealt with as a single group
g   description of the necessary expertise or skill

9 **Match the verbs 1–7 with verbs a–g that have a similar meaning.**

1 assure   a   need
2 fulfil   b   hope
3 participate   c   stop
4 prevent   d   promise
5 recommend   e   suggest
6 require   f   take part
7 trust   g   meet (requirements)

Now use the verbs 1–7 to complete the tender offer, which Marco (Vino Rubinetto) has written to Ines in response to the RFP on page 27.

Vino Rubinetto
Via Galileo Galilei 6
20161 Milano
Italia
Tel: +39 2 72 52 43 01
Fax +39 2 72 52 43 02
Mail: Falcone@vino-rubinetto.it
www.vino-rubinetto.it

Dear Ms Stoll

Your tender (no. 1238 HG) – Offer for sparkling red wine and prosecco

Thank you for inviting us to _____ [1] in the above bidding process.

I confirm that we can _____ [2] your requirements in regard to the requested low alcohol level of the sparkling red wine. The sparkling red wine will be produced in 2006 and the prosecco in 2009 and the EU quality level is 1. Both wines will be available for the next five years.

We strongly _____ [3] our dry prosecco, which I can _____ [4] you is not excessively dry. We are confident that your connoisseurs will agree.

We are currently able to deliver both products in our standard 750 ml green bottles. We will be able to meet your specifications of clear bottles by the summer of next year. We _____ [5] that this minor difference from your tender will not _____ [6] us from doing business together.

Our prices are:
Sparkling red wine:
€26.00 per bottle for a minimum purchase of 10,000 bottles
€27.00 per bottle for a minimum purchase of 5,000 bottles
€29.00 per bottle for a minimum purchase of 3,000 bottles

Prosecco (dry):
€24.00 per bottle for a minimum purchase of 10,000 bottles
€26.00 per bottle for a minimum purchase of 5,000 bottles
€27.50 per bottle for a minimum purchase of 3,000 bottles

Please feel free to contact me if you _____ [7] any further information.

We look forward to working with you.

Yours sincerely
Marco Falcone

10 **Ines has received Marco's offer and finds some differences with the requirements set out in the tender. Read through both documents again, then complete Ines's notes.**

Offer from
Marco, Vino Rubinetto Differences from specifications in our tender:
1) The prices are above our budget
2)
3)
4)

AUDIO
11

10

Now listen to this extract from the conversation between Ines and Marco. Which points do they discuss?

Listen again and complete the sentences.

Marco	_____ [1] clear bottles versus green?
Marco	_____ [2] Well, I have some good news on that.
Ines	So, _____ [3], you will be able to supply both wines in clear bottles as we requested.
Marco	_____ [4], yes.
Ines	Well, that's good. OK. The next thing is the price.
Marco	The price? _____ [5]?
Marco	Well, I did give you a range of prices depending on the quantity purchased ...
Ines	_____ [6]
Marco	... and 26 euros really is a good price.
Marco	But I'll see what I can do.
Ines	_____ [7] on that?
Ines	We need wines that are available for at least ten years.
Marco	_____.[8] And in our offer we said five years, _____ [9]?

ACTIVE LISTENING

You can communicate better by using active listening strategies. It is very important to continually check the information you receive to make sure you have understood correctly. You can do this using the following techniques:

Back-channeling – **showing that you are** **really listening**	**Prompting – asking for** **more information**	**Paraphrasing –** **making sure you have** **understood correctly**	**Confirming –** **saying that you have** **understood**
Mmmh, good.	Interesting. Could you	So you'd like ..., but only	That's correct, yes.
Yeah, OK.	tell me more about	if ... Is that right?	That's right.
Ah ah. I see.	that?	So, if I understand you	Yes, I see your point.
Right.	Yes, could you give me	correctly, you need ...	So, you'll get back to
	some more details?	Sorry, did you say ... ?	me on that.
	Would you be able to		
	provide more specific		
	information?		

---

12   **Work with a partner. Use the information in the Partner Files to have a telephone conversation. Look at your notes, and try to use active listening strategies when making your telephone call.**

PARTNER FILES ➤   Partner A   File 3, p. 60
Partner B   File 3, p. 62

OUTPUT

Look at the following opinions about open vs closed biddings and Internet auctions.

Open biddings are always the best because not only do we get the full range of what the market has to offer, but also the sales people compete with each other so we get the best price!

Open biddings are fun – they challenge my skills as a sales rep. I get to talk to the client's reps in order to find out exactly what they are looking for and what they are prepared to pay for it. Anything else is number crunching.

At my company we prefer closed biddings because we do not need a large number of offers. We have clear specifications and we are looking for partners that can match our standards.

Closed biddings are really hard. You need to build trust and you need to show consistent quality to be invited into a circle of potential suppliers.

Auctions via the Internet are my daily business – and it's great: no long talks and negotiations. Just a simple check of whether a supplier matches our specifications and the rest is an electronic ranking according to the price they offer.

Auctions on the Internet are a real pain when you compare them to other forms of bidding. There is hardly a chance for building trust because it is all so remote. And most client specifications are not as clear as the clients believe them to be.

OVER TO YOU

- Which statement can you most relate to? Which procedure do you prefer to work with?
- What types of offers are you usually involved in at your company? Would you prefer to change the way your company handles offers?
- How do you think your counterpart likes the way your company deals with offers?

4 Negotiations

Look at the tips below. First, work with a partner to add two tips of your own, then rank the tips from most important (1) to least important (10).

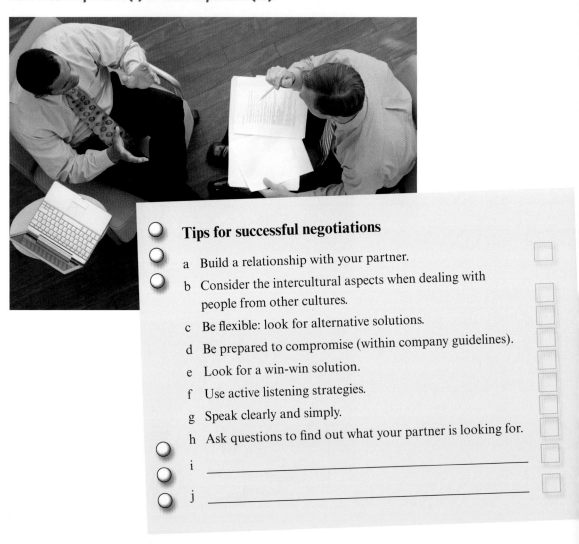

Tips for successful negotiations

a Build a relationship with your partner.

b Consider the intercultural aspects when dealing with people from other cultures.

c Be flexible: look for alternative solutions.

d Be prepared to compromise (within company guidelines).

e Look for a win-win solution.

f Use active listening strategies.

g Speak clearly and simply.

h Ask questions to find out what your partner is looking for.

i _____

j _____

Now discuss these questions with your partner.

1 How often do you negotiate in English? What kind of things do you negotiate (price, delivery dates, etc.)? Where are the people you negotiate with from (Europe, Asia, etc.)?

2 Do you usually agree terms and conditions over the phone, in person, or in writing? Which do you find easiest/most difficult? Why?

3 How do you follow up an agreement you make on the phone? Do you write confirmation emails or formal letters?

AUDIO
11

1 Gavin Brock, senior sales manager at Car Rental International in Paris, has sent an offer to Gabi Bernstein, senior purchaser at Euro Insurances Ltd in Frankfurt, and is now visiting her office to discuss the details. Listen to their conversation and decide which statement best describes the stage of their negotiation.

a   They are establishing their objectives.
b   They are negotiating specific parts of the offer.
c   They have reached agreement and are summarizing the next steps.

Listen again to the dialogue and complete Gavin's notes from the meeting with Gabi. What does Gavin need to do after the meeting?

> <u>Notes</u> — Meeting with Gabi Bernstein of Euro Insurances Ltd
>
> • Our offer is fairly <u>competitive</u> [1], but overall _____ [2] is too high.
> • Alternative offer, basically same conditions, but lower price.
>
> Main points from Gabi:
> • No _____ [3] fees for cars with right-hand drive for Britain and Ireland.
> • Suggestion, they take _____ [4] more cars for that region, we lower the offer by _____ [5] % (tax advantages).
> • Reduction in the overhead _____ [6] for repairs and maintenance. Special repair insurance, monthly fee?
> • Extend duration of contract by four years, another 5% price discount? 4% is probably our _____ [7].
>   New calculation, can we offer 5%?

2 Find words from the dialogue and Gavin's notes which mean the following.

1   the length of time something will last: _____

2   the amount of money you have to pay for a particular service: _____

3   something that is only temporary, not yet final: _____

4   the amount of money that is taken off the price: _____

5   the specific parts of a contract that both parties must agree to: _____

6   the process of using numbers to work out an amount: _____

Now use the correct form of the words from page 33 to complete these sentences.

a The board of directors has given us strict guidelines as to the _____ of contracts
we make with our partners. We cannot agree to a contract which runs for more than three years.

b We often give _____ to new customers and hope that we can then establish a long-
term relationship with them which will also benefit us in the long term.

c They've offered to lower their price if we buy the first 100 models within a month. Now we have to

do the _____ to see whether our storage costs would increase as a result.

d We have agreed to all the _____ of the contract, except the delivery dates. They will
make us a new offer next week.

e They want to charge us additional _____ for the maintenance of the units, but we
believe this should be included in the overall price.

f I've sent the _____ report to our client so that they can give it their approval.

DISCUSSING TERMS AND CONDITIONS

Conditional sentences are often used in sales negotiations to discuss terms and conditions. The type of
conditional sentence you use depends largely on the message you want to give.

To discuss facts and things which are always true, such as your standard terms and conditions:
***When** you **order** more than 100 articles, you **get** a five per cent discount.*

To discuss terms and conditions which you consider very possible:
***If** you **buy** more than 200 articles, we**'ll give** you a seven per cent discount.*
***If** we **buy** five more cars, we **will** also **need** a reduction in the overhead costs.*
A salesperson might use this form to make the offer more attractive for the buyer, or the buyer might use it
to stress a condition they feel strongly about.

To discuss terms and conditions which are less likely, or to show that you are just looking into possibilities:
***If** you **took** just five more cars, we **could lower** our offer by five per cent.*
***If** we **extended** the contract, **would** you **provide** us with a five per cent discount?*
This form is often used to see how far the other party is willing to go in a negotiation, without making any
promises yourself. It is less direct and thus comes across as more polite.

AUDIO
12–16

3 **Listen to the following sentences and decide which speakers are talking about:**

a conditions which are facts or always true.

_____

b terms and conditions that are very possible

for both partners. _____

c possibilities which both partners are

considering. _____

4   Complete the following conditional sentences with the correct form of the verbs in brackets. Use the hints in the bubbles to help you choose the correct form.

1   If we _____ (lease) our entire fleet from them,

we _____ (receive) a big reduction in the overall costs.

looking at possibilities

2   If you _____ (increase) the order by just 50,

we _____ (can lower) our offer by five per cent.

making the offer more attractive

3   If we _____ (agree) to your payment schedule,

we _____ (need) a reduction in the overall costs.

stressing an important condition

4   If you _____ (agree) to all the other conditions, then I'm sure

we _____ (be able to) meet your demands for the delivery times.

looking at possibilities

5   When you _____ (buy) our inspection services for a monthly fee,

you _____ (receive) a discount for the maintenance fees.

fact, always true

6   If we _____ (extend) the duration of the contract by another four

years, _____ you _____ (reduce) the overall price by five per cent?

looking at possibilities

7   If it _____ (be) all right with you, I _____ (send)

you the draft version of the contract by Wednesday.

very possible

5   Work with a partner. Choose some of the situations below – or think of your own from your job – and write conditional sentences to fit the situation.

1   *A*   You are meeting with long-term clients who have not bought anything from you for the last year. You want to offer them a discount on their next order.
    B   You have found a new supplier who is less expensive than A's company. They can also guarantee shorter delivery times.

2   *A*   You know that this supplier has difficulties in delivering on time. But for a guaranteed delivery time, you will pay more.
    B   You have storage problems, and sometimes have to wait for your own suppliers. Therefore you do not want to guarantee delivery times to your customers. Can you get them to order more in order to reduce the price?

3   *A*   You are talking to an important client of yours. Offer him or her a special price or discount on condition that they sign a five-year leasing contract.
    B   Your company is in a restructuring process, and therefore you cannot agree to a long-term contract. You do, however, want to get a reduction because you have found another potential supplier.

6   **Rachel Cohen, assistant key account manager at the Building Rental Society, is meeting Laura Vialli, a buyer at Café Europa, a franchising company for cafés. They are negotiating the conditions for renting property in London.**

Listen to the extract and say whether the following sentences are true ✔ or false ✗.

a   Laura feels that the price for leasing the property is too high.

b   Rachel refuses to consider a shorter leasing period because there is a lot of interest in the property from other buyers.

c   Rachel is willing to offer a lower leasing rate in exchange for a percentage of the café's turnover.

Listen again to the dialogue and complete the extracts with the missing words or phrases.

1   Well, compared to the other offers we've received so far, it's certainly _____.

2   Yes, I agree. That _____ to offer you a better price, which I'm sure is in your

_____, isn't it?

3   Ah, I _____ your difficulty.

4   Normally we _____ that, but I think we also need to consider …

5   You _____ there, but the leasing period is an extremely important factor in setting our price.

6   I'm sorry. I'm _____. What exactly are you proposing?

7   If the café is the success we are all hoping for, it will be _____ to both you and us.

Would that be _____?

8   That _____, but I would have to talk to my boss about it and get back to you.

NEGOTIATING STYLES

Remember that negotiating styles differ not only from person to person, but also across cultures. There are many factors which may influence how your partner behaves, so be prepared for situations which might not be typical in your country. For example, when meeting business partners from Britain or the U.S.A., negotiations normally allow time for small talk at the beginning. Even in formal meetings or negotiations, it is felt that relationship-building can ensure a successful outcome.

Differences may also occur from industry to industry. IT people are usually much more relaxed in their clothing and behaviour than, for example, bankers, and this will probably be reflected in their negotiating style.

When negotiating with partners from other cultures, do your homework. Get acquainted with the customs, manners and conventions as well as some of the dos and don'ts.

7 After the meeting, Laura writes the following email to the head of her department. Complete the gaps with the correct form of the verbs below.

> accept • differ • enable • offer • receive • reduce • suggest

Hello Franco,

As you know, after _____ [1] various offers for rental premises in London, I am in the negotiation phase with the better agents. My impression is that the leasing period in London is quite standard; the terms that they have _____ [2] do not _____ [3] much.

One offer was a bit different though. Rachel from Building Rental Society _____ [4] a leasing rate partly based on our turnover at the premises. Could we _____ [5] this, depending, of course, on the percentage rate itself? It would _____ [6] us to _____ [7] the fixed price quite considerably.

Please let me know what you think.

Thanks
Laura

8 Look at these ways to agree or disagree with someone. Put a tick ✔ next to the ones which mean agreement and a cross ✗ next to those which mean disagreement.

a I see it a little differently. ✗

b I share your views completely. ✓

c That may well be right, but …

d We could go along with that.

e Up to a point we could accept that, but …

f I really can't agree with that.

g Yes, I'm absolutely in favour of that option.

h I agree.

i Normally we could accept that, but in this case …

j Unfortunately, I can't agree with you there.

Now use the expressions a–j from page 37 to respond to the following statements. Note that sometimes more than one answer is possible.

1 A This is going to be a very big order so it's important we get everything right.

   B _h_____ . We'll do the calculations and get back to you.

2 A I think it's important we look at the big picture. Hopefully we can create a win-win situation.

   B _____ . It really is best for both of us if we can establish a successful long-term relationship.

3 A I'm sure you'll see that the increased price is not such a big issue.

   B _____ . The overall price is the most important point for us.

4 A Let me see if I've understood. You would actually prefer to pay higher prices if we can guarantee the delivery times?

   B _____ . If we can be sure that deliveries are always on time, then we can pass on some extra costs to our clients.

5 A You know, this is the standard practice here in Japan.

   B _____ , but in this case we think that the size of our order should convince you to change your standard practice.

AUDIO
18

9 **Gavin Brock from Car Rental International is having a second meeting with his client, Gabi Bernstein, from Euro Insurances Ltd. Listen to the conversation and tick ✔ the sentences you hear.**

1 a We would like to create a long-term partnership. ☐
   b A long-term partnership is best for both of us. ☐

2 a That is certainly interesting for us. ☐
   b That is certainly in our best interests. ☐

3 a But it is necessary that both parties benefit for that to work. ☐
   b However, both parties have to benefit for that to work. ☐

4 a I'm happy we've found a solution. ☐
   b I'm glad we've been able to find a solution. ☐

Do they manage to reach agreement on their contract for leasing company cars?
What are the conditions?
Would this conversation count as a legally binding agreement in your country?
Why, or why not?

WIN-WIN NEGOTIATIONS

In a negotiation, both parties are looking to get the best result for their company. You can use the phrases below to show your partner that what you are offering will be good for them.

*We're sure it would also be **in your best interest(s)**.*
*It would be **to your advantage to** ...*
*You will be able to reduce overall costs **in the long term**.*

Many negotiation experts have suggested that parties should look for solutions where both will benefit – this is called the 'win-win' situation. Here are some phrases which may help you achieve this.

***Both parties must benefit** for that to work.*
*That is **best for both of us**.*
*We would like to create **a long-term partnership**.*

10   **Complete Gavin's email to Gabi with words from the box. Does the email mention everything that was agreed?**

appreciated • confirm • continuing • down payment • fee • opportunity • reach • summarize

Dear Gabi

Thank you for our constructive meeting yesterday. I _____ [1] the opportunity to meet with you again, and I am glad we were able to _____ [2] agreement. As promised, I'm writing to _____ [3] the points we have discussed so far.

1. We will not include additional fees for the cars with right-hand drive for Britain and Ireland if you take five more cars in that region.

2. You will take our special insurance offer for a monthly _____ [4]. It includes the annual overhaul and the mounting of winter tyres.

3. You agreed to extend the duration of the contract by four years.

4. You agreed to make a _____ [5] of a third of the annual turnover within seven days of signing the contract.

5. We will take advantage of the one-day registration laws in Germany, and offer the cars to you as used cars.

6. If all of the above points are agreed, then we will reduce our overall offer by six per cent.

Please contact me to _____ [6] that you agree with these points. I will then get our lawyers to draft a contract for your consideration.

Once again, thank you for the _____ [7] to work with you on this. I look forward to _____ [8] our cooperation over the next few years.

Yours sincerely
Gavin Brock

11   Review the phrases used in the unit as well as the ones in the box below. Then work with a partner. Use the role cards in the Partner Files or think up your own situation to negotiate and try to reach an agreement with your partner.

PARTNER FILES   Partner A   File 4, p. 60
Partner B   File 4, p. 62

NEGOTIATION LANGUAGE

Starting the conversation
We're very happy to be meeting you today.
We hope to come to an acceptable solution for both of us.
I'd like to discuss some of the details in the offer.
We'd like to hear your proposals before we tell you what we can offer.

Concluding your arguments
So that wraps it up.
That sums up our side then.
We are sure that you will see the benefits for your company if you take up our offer.
There you have our proposal. I'm afraid that's as far as we can go.

Finishing the conversation
That may be a possibility, but I have to discuss it with my boss.
Let me get back to you.
I'm happy we've found a solution. I'll send you an email tomorrow summarizing
    our agreement.

---

12   One word in each of the lines below does not go with the item in bold. Cross out the word that does not fit, as in the example.

1   offer   ~~order~~   negotiate   get   **a discount**
2   agree to   guarantee   reduce   move up   **a delivery date**
3   lower   extend   reduce   agree to   **the duration of a contract**
4   accept   reconsider   receive   calculate   **an offer**
5   reduce   increase   extend   lower   **the price**
6   **guarantee**   quality   delivery times   a contract   cheaper prices
7   **negotiate**   the price   the conditions   an offer   a relationship

13   Complete the table with nouns from the unit.

VERB	NOUN	VERB	NOUN
to increase	1	to propose	6
to discuss	2	to calculate	7
to benefit	3	to sign	8
to differ	4	to reduce	9
to summarize	5	to extend	10

Do you have any experience with auctions? Do you think they can replace direct negotiations? Read the following article and discuss the questions which follow.

http://www.report.com

| The Auction | Search | Notes | Forums | Links | Shop |

⇨ Topic of the week: **The Auction**

Going, going, gone!

We asked two of our regular contributors to tell us what they think the role of auctions is in today's marketplace.

Willem van Haart, Sales Director at Trimmens Electric

Auctions have been part of sales for as long as there has been anything to sell. Think of a market in Tunisia, for example, where they sell freshly-caught fish to the highest bidder every day, or high-profile auction houses like Sotheby's, where paintings are sold for outrageous sums.

But for most of us, auctions are just not part of our daily business, and never will be. The products or services we sell are not in such high demand that buyers are willing to fight each other for them. Most sellers need to do it the hard way: knocking on doors, making a sales pitch to potential customers and negotiating the terms and conditions. Auctions may be a part of life in some industries, but they will never replace personal negotiations. Selling happens between people, in face-to-face communication!

Jennifer Ramirez, Head of European Purchasing at Northern Oil

It is true that sales auctions are nothing new, but it is unusual for purchasers to hold auctions. In the oil industry where I work, there are usually quite a large number of potential suppliers and we decided we could get better conditions if we started to auction our contracts. At the beginning we did have some problems. For example, it was sometimes difficult to compare offers because the suppliers offered different packages in terms of quality, quantity, delivery time, etc. We have had to work with both our internal departments and our suppliers to make sure the offers have the same parameters.

And the future of auctions? I think they will be used more frequently – sometimes as an alternative to negotiations, mostly as an additional tool. Although it takes a little more time to prepare for an auction, the process is cheaper and provides better results – for purchasers! Sales reps hate it. Their whole planning is about building relationships that can make up for any price disadvantages and hopefully bind a client to them as firmly as possible.

DID YOU KNOW?

Auctions

We all know auctions as a structured sales process in which potential buyers bid for a product or service, whether in person, over the telephone, via letters or by email. In recent years, e-auctions – where bidders participate online via an Internet platform – have become more widespread.

The term 'English auction' refers to the style of an auction, whether traditional or online. The bidding starts with the lowest offer from a potential buyer and ends with the highest offer. A 'Dutch auction' is the opposite. Here the seller quotes a high price, then the asking price is gradually lowered until one of the buyers is willing to pay. Finally, a 'reverse auction' is a bidding process conducted by purchasers, where the suppliers bid for a contract.

OVER TO YOU

- What are the advantages and disadvantages of both auctions and direct negotiations?
- Do you (or would you) prefer auctions or more direct negotiations with your business partners? Why?
- Which are more common in your line of business and why?

5 Orders

Discuss these questions with a partner.

1 How often do you place/take an order? Do you mostly deal with companies in your country or abroad?
2 What are the steps involved in placing/taking an order for your company? What forms do you have to complete?
3 Do you need approval from your superiors to place/take all orders, or just for ones involving large quantities or significant amounts of money?
4 When working with foreign companies, what are the most difficult aspects in placing/taking orders?

AUDIO
19–20

1 **Jean Duban works as a salesperson for the international telecommunications supplier TEGID (SA) in Lyon, and spends a lot of time on the phone. Listen to two of his phone conversations and complete the notes.**

> Customer Order:
> from Junko Hanamura, JapanCom in _____ 1
> Quantity: model # XPR14: _____ 2
>   model # _____ 3: 250
> Delivery by Friday morning to _____ 4
> Need to fax _____ 5 contract

> Customer Order:
> from Alex Beck, Phone Europe, Sheffield
> First order under the _____ 6 contract
> Quantity: _____ 7 extension leads
> Delivery within _____ 8 months

AUDIO
19–20

2 **Listen to the calls again and complete the sentences below.**

Call 1

1 We _____ some USB adapters for our network.

2 Can you _____ to our office in Osaka by Friday morning?

3 So, let me _____ I've got everything down right.

4 Fine. _____ a model contract immediately.

Call 2

5 ... we're _____ our first order under the frame contract.

6 Let me just find a pen so I can _____ .

7 Of course. I'll email it to you _____ .

8 I _____ to let you know how things are going.

EXCHANGING INFORMATION

When handling orders, it is important for the salesperson and the purchaser to exchange all relevant information such as:

- Specifications (for material, quality, etc.)
- Quantity
- Contact person
- Place of delivery
- Delivery date
- Method of payment (e.g. cash on delivery (COD), invoice, direct debit)
- Other terms and conditions
- Paperwork needed (signed order, confirmation by fax, etc.)

Much of the information above is included in a *frame contract*. Also called a *call-off purchase agreement*, this type of contract is often drawn up when a client or company needs a just-in-time delivery of standard products that they do not want to store themselves. An order placed under a frame contract is called a *call-off order*.

---

3 **Complete the sentences with words and phrases from the box.**

delivery • frame contract • invoice • method of payment • place of delivery • shipment • signed order • specifications

1 We'd like to place our first order in accordance with the terms and conditions of our _____

   _____ . The _____ will be our warehouse near Coventry.

2 We've sent the _____ to your factory. The _____ is enclosed and should

   be paid within 30 days of _____ .

3 We've spoken to our production unit, and I can assure you that we will be able to meet all the

   _____ of your order.

4 Our charges depend on your chosen _____. You'll find details of how you can pay for the goods on our website.

5 As soon as we have received your _____ (or returned email confirmation), we will pass your order on to the production unit.

4 **Work with a partner. Use the information in the Partner Files to practise handling orders. Try to use some of the phrases from the box below.**

PARTNER FILES
Partner A   File 5, p. 61
Partner B   File 5, p. 63

HANDLING ORDERS

Placing orders
We would like to order/have …
We're ready to make our first order under the frame contract.
We'd like to place a call-off order for 3,000 units.
We would appreciate delivery by Friday. Can you manage it/that?

Taking orders
I'll just take/write down the details.
Let me just write this down/type in your order.
So, how many do you need exactly?
Was there anything else you'd like to order today?

Checking and confirming information
Let me just check/repeat that.
Let me make sure I've got everything down right.
Yes, that's right/correct.
Sorry. Did you say …?
Could you say that again/repeat that, please?

---

5 **Anna Long works as a purchaser at Stores International in Leeds. She has just placed an order under a new frame contract with their wholesaler Fashion Modes Plc in Milan. Look at the web order on the next page, and use the words below to complete the gaps.**

a VAT
b Contact
c Total value of goods
d Delivery addresses
e Gross
f Invoice
g Place of delivery

You have just completed this order. Please check all items before confirming.

Client	Stores International, Leeds, England
Frame contract	128qjg978
Order number	WC0001-128jh
Authorization (PIN)	********************
_____ / _____ [1]	T: +44 (211) 5560-900 E: A.Long@stores-international.com
Payment terms	_____ [2] payable within 30 days upon delivery
Billing address	Stores International c/o Anna Long 40 North Street Leeds, England
_____ [3]	Central warehouses, addresses known

No.	Item	Part number	Size	Quantity	Description	Price per item	Total price	Date of delivery	_____ [4]
001	Shirt (men)	SM-12B	M	2000	white, button down	3.00	6,000.00	9 Nov	Leeds
002	T-shirt (men)	TM-34J	L	5000	white	1.00	5,000.00	9 Nov	Manchester
003	Sweat shirt	SW-87H	L	1500	grey, black, blue	3.50	5,250.00	9 Nov	London
004	Jeans (men)	JM-15T	52	2000	stone washed blue	5.00	10,000.00	9 Nov	London
005	Blouse	BL-84G	M	3000	pink	3.00	9,000,00	9 Nov	Manchester
006	T-shirt (women)	TW-34Z	S	2500	light blue	1.00	2,500.00	9 Nov	Leeds
007	Skirt	SK-43H	36	1000	red & blue	5.00	5,000.00	9 Nov	Birmingham

_____ [5] (net)	42,750.00
Currency	euro
_____ [6] (19%)	8,122.50
_____ [7] (total price)	**50,872.50**

Send

Comments: Please make sure that all items are accompanied by detailed delivery notes.

After completion of the order you will receive an automatic confirmation via email. Should you not receive this email within one hour, please contact our international hotline 1-800-09111959.

REFERRING TO NUMBERS ON AN ORDER

In sales and purchasing, the terms *part number*, *item number*, and *article number* are often used interchangeably. A more technical term is *SKU, stock-keeping unit*. Like the other terms above, this sequence of numbers and/or letters is used to refer to and identify a specific product for both sales and inventory purposes.

Note that the abbreviation for *number* is *no*. (or sometimes #).

6   Use the clues to complete the crossword puzzle.
You can find all the answers on the form on page 45.

Across
2 USD, EUR, and GBP are examples of this.
5 The form that the supplier fills in and sends with the goods.
7 The person at the other company who you should talk to.

Down
1 How the money for the goods should be paid.
2 FCMIONNATRIO: *I'll send written …*
3 The building where goods are stored.
4 17.5% in the U.K.
6 How much the goods are worth.

AUDIO
21

7   Anna now has to change her order. She calls her contact at Fashion Modes, the sales rep Roberto Branca. Listen to their conversation and decide whether the following are true ☑ or false ☒ .

1 The online tool for changing orders doesn't work yet.

2 Anna will automatically receive an email confirming the changes.

3 Anna wants to make two changes to the order.

8   Listen again to the conversation, and tick ☑ the sentences and phrases you hear.

1 I need to change the order …

2 I'll make a note of the changes.

3 I'll need written confirmation as well.

4 I'll enter the changes into the system …

5 … could you please tell me the order number?

6 Could you tell me which items are incorrect?

7 It ought to be Brighton, not Birmingham.

8 … could I also ask you to add another item to the order?

Now decide which of these sentences you can use to:

a change an order. *1,* _____

b accept a change to an order. *2,* _____

9 **Use sentences from exercise 8 to complete the following mini-dialogues.**

A What will happen now? I mean, I need some sort of confirmation.

B Yes, of course. _____ ¹, and you'll automatically receive a confirmation email.

A Unfortunately one of the items is incorrect, and I need to change it. Can you do that for me?

B Of course. It's no problem. But first, _____ ²

A _____ ³

B Of course, I can take care of that for you. What would you like to change?

A _____ ⁴

B Yes, of course. I'll send you an email straight away so you can see what we've changed.

A I'm sorry, but I need to talk to you about some mistakes in our order number 07/345.

B Yes, certainly. _____ ⁵

A _____ ⁶

B Yes, of course. We're always happy to increase the order.

AUDIO
22

10 **Sometimes it can be difficult to understand numbers and figures given over the phone. Listen to the recordings and complete the missing information.**

1 The order number is _____. Have you got that?

2 Sales have been great. So far this year we've sold a total of _____ units. That's an increase of _____ over last year.

3 Good news. We can save up to _____ each quarter if we switch suppliers.

4 I'm pleased to report that this facility was able to increase output from _____ to _____ last quarter.

5 I have a question about one of the items you ordered. It's item number _____, the _____ cable.

6 The net total for your latest order is _____. With the Dutch VAT of _____, this gives you a gross total of _____.

11 **Review the phrases on page 44 for checking and confirming information. Now work with a partner. Use the information in the Partner Files to practise passing on figures over the phone.**

PARTNER FILES   Partner A File 6, p. 61
Partner B File 6, p. 63

12   Here are some extracts from a standard contract between Phone Europe in Sheffield and their French supplier, TEGID (SA). Match the two parts to make contract terms.

1	binding	a	and regulations
2	liable	b	of the contract
3	due	c	on arrears
4	interest	d	all rights
5	invalidate any other clauses	e	agreement
6	reserves	f	date
7	revoke	g	this contract
8	subject matter	h	for any damages

Now complete these extracts from the contract with the contract terms above.

The _____ [1] is the delivery of electronic equipment by TEGID (SA) to Phone Europe. (For specifications of conditions, delivery terms and dates, see Appendix A. Unless otherwise provided these specifications are binding to both contracting parties.)

The signature of both contracting parties constitutes a _____ [2] for the delivery of the chosen articles; call-off orders will be handled through the online portal of TEGID (SA). Both sides accept the general standard terms and conditions of TEGID (SA).

TEGID (SA) _____ [3] to select suitable logistical partners to meet scheduled delivery dates. TEGID (SA) is not _____ [4] or losses incurred by the logistical partners.

Phone Europe agrees to fulfil its payment obligation within 14 calendar days after receipt of the articles. If the contracting party exceeds the _____ [5] by more then ten calendar days, TEGID (SA) will charge an _____ [6] of four per cent above the base interest rate of the European Central Bank. €10 will be charged for each reminder.

An agreement clause being or becoming void does not _____ [7].

TEGID (SA) reserves all rights to _____ [8] in parts or in full if Phone Europe infringes any of the agreed provisions. A penalty depends on the extent of the damage incurred by TEGID (SA) (for details see Appendix B).

13 A colleague at TEGID (SA) asks questions about the contract. Can you give an answer?

1 'When does Phone Europe need to pay by? And what happens if they pay late? Will they have to pay interest?'

2 'We can't accept this clause. If we strike it out, will they have to draw up a new contract, or is it still valid?'

3 'Who will actually deliver the goods? And what happens if a third party causes damage to the goods?'

4 'Under what circumstances can we get out of the contract?'

OUTPUT Look at the following comments about using integrated business software for processing and tracking orders. Which opinion(s) do you agree with?

Judy Welsh, Head of Sales
Using electronic ordering systems is really great. Everything is so much quicker and easier. I remember when we used to send orders by fax. First you had to type up the order, then print it out, and pray the fax machine was working. Now everything is done by computer. It's wonderful.

Ken Fellows, Key Account Manager
Working with online ordering systems is a pain. They are so complicated and much too detailed. Plus, I prefer to deal with real people rather than websites, emails, and paper, anyway. It makes business more fun and it is also faster.

Lee Park, Buyer
What really gets on my nerves are websites where I place an order and then I don't get any response, nothing – no message, no email – telling me that the order is actually being processed. That's when I reach for the phone or write an email of my own so I can make sure that my order has really been received.

Anna Jones, Sales Rep
Electronic tools should be just that: tools. They are just there to make life easier and shouldn't be used to do the things people can do better. If you blame the tool when things go wrong, then you just aren't doing your job right.

OVER TO YOU

- Have you ever used an integrated business system to handle orders? What do you think the advantages and disadvantages are?
- Have you ever encountered any problems with an automated system for placing or taking an order? Describe what happened. How do you think this type of problem can be avoided?

6 Customer care

Look at the following list of problems which have been mentioned by people working in sales and purchasing. Tick ☑ the ones which you have personally had to deal with. Can you add any other problems to the lists?

What salespeople complain about:

Orders are often cancelled at the last moment. ☐

Customers sometimes pay late (or not at all). ☐

Customers often send incomplete order forms. ☐

_____ ☐

What purchasers complain about:

There are often delays in delivery. ☐

The wrong goods are sometimes sent. ☐

The quality of the product is often not as we expect. ☐

_____ ☐

Work with a partner. Choose a problem from the lists above. Imagine somebody is complaining to you about it. How might you respond?

AUDIO
23–24

1 Two customers are making complaints. Listen to these extracts from the phone calls and complete the table.

	Problem	Solution
Call 1		
Call 2		

Match the two parts to make sentences from the dialogues. Then listen again to check your answers.

1 There seems to be a
2 Sorry, but I need something
3 Can you manage delivery
4 I can confirm that
5 I'm afraid that
6 Somebody should have
7 I'll personally get
8 Can you confirm that

a more specific so I can tell our customers.
b it's still not working correctly.
c mistake with the shipment.
d someone will be here by noon?
e fixed the problem yesterday.
f by Friday?
g on to the service unit immediately ...
h you'll receive the sensors first thing Friday morning.

COMPLAINING EFFECTIVELY

When making a complaint, it is helpful to use the following three-step approach:
1 Describe the problem.
2 State your request clearly (what, when, how, who).
3 Confirm agreements.

We use certain words and phrases in English to make a complaint less aggressive and personal:
> **I'm afraid** (that) there is a problem with ...
> **There appears / seems to be** a mistake / mix-up ...
> **Unfortunately**, we have a **slight** problem with ...

We can also use sentences with *should have* to explain exactly what went wrong:
> Somebody **should have fixed** the problem yesterday.
> The shipment **should have been sent** to Shanghai, not Seoul.
> We **should have received** the delivery last week.

There seems to be a mistake. I didn't order candles.

AUDIO
23–24

2 **Listen to the phone calls in exercise 1 again (or look at the transcripts on pages 74–75.) Do the speakers follow the three-step approach above when making their complaints? Find examples.**

3 **Put the words in the right order to make sentences used to make complaints. Note that in each case there is one word you do not need.**

1 the invoice with there's I'm afraid a problem that seems
2 appears I'm this delay will afraid cause problems us
3 haven't received already shipment We the yet
4 to shipment should The been sent Moscow received have
5 should Unfortunately is still the program not working
6 for can understand this I is frustrating slight you that
7 you confirm that here unfortunately someone will be tomorrow? Can
8 technicians could yesterday Your should have fixed it
9 mistake to be Unfortunately manage seems a the order with there

AUDIO

25

4   Linda Matthews, a purchaser at Logistics International, is ringing Alena Novák, a sales rep at Paper 4 U in Prague. Listen to their conversation and take notes. What is the problem and what action will Alena take to fix the problem?

5   Listen again to the dialogue between Linda and Alena and complete the sentences.

1   Right, I _____ .

2   I realize this is _____ so I'll see to it immediately.

3   _____ you a few questions first?

4   What _____ by 'the wrong paper'?

5   I _____ with Production and arrange a special delivery …

6   I _____ the shipment is at your location no later than 10 a.m. tomorrow.

7   I'll _____ make sure you get the right paper tomorrow.

Which of the above sentences can be used to:

a   confirm that you have understood the client's situation? _____

b   ask for details of the problem? _____

c   suggest solutions to the problem? _____

d   help the client by confirming what has been agreed? _____

COMPLAINT MANAGEMENT WITH *CASH*

When dealing with complaints, it is helpful to follow a four-step approach:

Confirm that you have understood the client's situation and can see why he or she is angry or frustrated. (Note that we sometimes say sorry even though something is not our fault.)
  I'm sorry to hear that. / I understand your situation.
  I realize this must be frustrating for you.

Ask for the details of the problem and find out what the customer has already tried to do to solve the problem.
  Could you tell me exactly which item was damaged?
  May I ask if you've tried to use the tracking facility on our website?

Serve your client by suggesting solutions that are as quick and easy as possible.
  You will get the missing shipment within 24 hours.
  I'll get back to you first thing tomorrow morning about compensation.

Help your client by confirming your commitments and repeating what you agreed to do.
  I'll see to it immediately and personally make sure you get compensation.
  Are we agreed that you'll fax me a copy of the invoice and I'll send you the missing items today?

6   **Change these sentences so that they fit the CASH approach to customer care. Use the prompts in brackets.**

1   Is that really such a problem for you? (understand)   *I understand that is a problem for you.*
2   I guess that must be difficult. (realize)
3   What's the problem? (exactly)
4   Is that all right with you? (convenient)
5   So I think you'll get it next week. (make sure)
6   Someone will sort it out immediately. (I personally)
7   You'll hear from us soon about the discount. (I/on Friday)

7   **Complete the sentences with *will* (*'ll*) and verbs from the box.**

1   I ___*'ll see to*___ it immediately.
2   I _____ you get the shipment on time.
3   We _____ the order to your offices by Friday.
4   I _____ you the order form straight away.
5   I _____ the details and our agreement in writing.
6   You _____ the right goods tomorrow at the latest.

> confirm • deliver • fax •
> make sure • receive • ~~see to~~

8   **Work with a partner. Use a situation below or think of your own situation. Then use the flowchart to make dialogues. Use the phrases in the unit so far to make and respond to the complaints.**

Where is the contract? It should have been here last week.

The components you delivered are faulty. We've had to stop production!

The shipment is not here yet. Our customers won't be happy about delay.

We have not received the signed contract yet. We can't deliver until it arrives.

Payment is late again. We may have to stop the next delivery.

Tell S what is wrong.

Confirm that you have understood. Ask for details.

Give details and state your request.

Suggest a solution.

Reject the solution.

Agree to the solution and repeat what you've agreed.

Confirm.

P = purchaser   S = seller

9   Linda Matthews has a problem with a Dutch IT firm called Instant Solutions, and has filled out the complaint form on their website. Look at the form and say whether the following statements are true ☑ or false ☒ .

1   There is no frame contract related to this order.
2   Ineke de Bruin took the order.
3   After placing the order, Linda received an email confirming the shipment and delivery date.
4   Five items were missing from the order.
5   Ineke de Bruin has agreed to pay compensation.

Complaint Form

Client data:

Client (company, department):	Logistics International, Central Purchasing Dept.,
Representative (surname, first name):	Matthews, Linda
Address:	64 Clyde Road, Glasgow, Scotland
Email address:	linda.matthews@logint.com
Telephone number:	+ 44 (0) 342 04 57 68
Fax number:	+ 44 (0) 342 04 57 69

Shipment data:

Type of article:	Notebook NB 1005511
Number of items:	thirty
Order number:	NB1005511
Frame contract:	LIGFC 25230 of 10 February 2009
Shipment tracking number:	LI 342-4IFG

Type of request:

☒ Information about scheduled shipment | Shipment behind schedule ▼ |

☒ Delivery of wrong article | Article missing ▼ |

☐ Delivered article not fully functioning

☐ Defective article

☐ Documents incomplete

☐ Other requests: | ... ▼ |

Description:

I placed the order two weeks ago with Ms Ineke de Bruin. She sent an email a day later confirming the shipment 'as agreed', but there was no written confirmation of the delivery date. We should have received 30 of your notebooks as specified in the order mentioned above. We only received 25 notebooks, and they were two days late. To date we have received no information about the missing notebooks. This is the second time this has happened! We expect the missing items in the next few days plus compensation for the inconvenience caused.

---

10   Complete the table with words from the online form above.

VERB	NOUN		VERB	NOUN	
describe		1	inform		4
compensate		2	deliver		5
confirm		3	ship		6

Now use the correct form of words from the table to complete the sentences.

1   Their website is full of useful _____. Everything I wanted to know was available and easy to find.

2   We have _____ the order by special air courier. You will receive it in the morning.

3   Can you please _____ that in writing?

4   Could you _____ exactly what you have received?

5   I'm afraid we are unable to _____ that model until next week.

6   The frame contract provides _____ if the goods are not here on time.

11   **Ineke de Bruin of Instant Solutions has written the following email to Linda Matthews. What phrases does Ineke de Bruin use to:**

1   apologize?
2   show that she understands her customer's situation?
3   explain what caused the problem?
4   state what will be done to fix the problem?
5   offer another benefit to her customer?
6   apologize again?

Dear Linda,

Please accept my apologies for the late delivery of your notebooks. I very much regret the frustration and problems this has caused you.

Please be assured that we are doing everything to make sure that the missing notebooks arrive as soon as possible. The delay was caused by unexpected computer problems in our production department, which have since been resolved. The missing items will be delivered by special courier to your offices in Glasgow by Thursday at the latest.

Since this has happened for the second time and also as a sign of goodwill, I would like to offer you a free maintenance check of the PCs you have leased from us for your offices in Warsaw.

Again I regret the inconvenience and hope that we will be able to continue to do business together.

Should there be any further difficulties, please contact me directly so that I can personally take care of any problems.

Best regards,

Ineke de Bruin

PS: I'll call you on Friday to make sure everything is as it should be.

12   **Choose the most suitable word to complete these sentences.**

1   I apologize/regret/explain the inconvenience and hope that we will be able to do business together.

2   If you do not comply/obey/follow with the delivery terms as agreed, we will be sorry/forced/happy to find another supplier.

3   Please be assured/happy/satisfied that we are doing everything we can to fix the problem.

4   We will be made/forced/required to ask for compensation in this case.

5   We are writing to definitely/completely/formally complain about the situation.

6   Should there be any further difficulties, please inform me directly/first/quickly .

13   **Work with a partner. Read the following complaints, and discuss how you would deal with them. Then choose one and write a response. Try to use the phrases you have learned in this unit.**

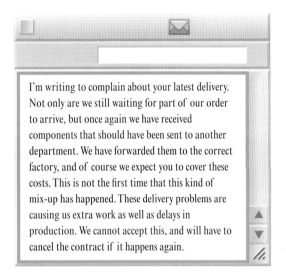

I'm writing to complain about your latest delivery. Not only are we still waiting for part of our order to arrive, but once again we have received components that should have been sent to another department. We have forwarded them to the correct factory, and of course we expect you to cover these costs. This is not the first time that this kind of mix-up has happened. These delivery problems are causing us extra work as well as delays in production. We cannot accept this, and will have to cancel the contract if it happens again.

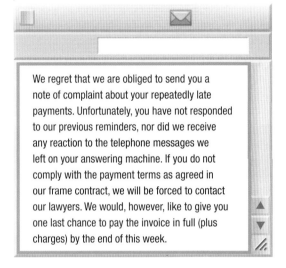

We regret that we are obliged to send you a note of complaint about your repeatedly late payments. Unfortunately, you have not responded to our previous reminders, nor did we receive any reaction to the telephone messages we left on your answering machine. If you do not comply with the payment terms as agreed in our frame contract, we will be forced to contact our lawyers. We would, however, like to give you one last chance to pay the invoice in full (plus charges) by the end of this week.

14   **Work with a partner. Use the information in the Partner Files and language from the unit to make and respond to complaints.**

PARTNER FILES   Partner A   File 7, p. 61
Partner B   File 7, p. 63

LETTERS OF COMPLAINT AND APOLOGY

Making complaints
I'm writing to you to complain about …
I am writing in reference to the above order.
   Unfortunately, …

Talking about consequences
We expect you to cover these costs.
We expect compensation for the inconvenience
   caused.
We cannot accept this and will have to cancel our
   contract if it happens again.
If you do not comply with the delivery terms as
   agreed in our frame contract, we will be forced to
   contact our lawyers.

Offering apologies
Please accept my apologies for …
Please be assured that we are doing everything …
I (very much) regret the inconvenience we have
   caused.

Referring to future action
We will, of course, cover the extra costs/reimburse
   you/arrange for a new shipment …
As a sign of goodwill, I would like to offer …

OUTPUT Read the following transcript from a speech which Cristina Pimenta, a senior sales rep at an international coffee-producing company, gave at her company's annual sales conference. Do you agree with the points she makes? Why, or why not?

+++ News and views from the annual sales conference +++

Cristina Pimenta

Our figures show that we are excellent at convincing new clients of the quality of our products. Yet figures for retaining clients – especially those very critical clients in Southern Europe – are … well … poor. We lose too many customers, and we all know what that means: winning a new client is much harder and a lot more expensive than keeping an existing one.

So our goal for the coming year is to improve the quality of our after-sales services. For that purpose we have developed three guiding principles.

1 We solve our clients' problems!

That means we try to understand their business needs. We find out what their problems are. We actively search for solutions. We surprise them. We think from the point of view of their clients – what they expect or will expect, what they want and how our partners can meet those expectations. If we can do that, our clients will love us and our products.

2 We search for the 'WE'!

This is what we should always look for. Whenever our clients think 'we', they are satisfied with our products and services. It means they are not looking for alternative suppliers. 'We' is the key signal for the quality of our relationship.

3 We turn our clients into winners.

When they win, we win. It's as simple as that. Our clients want to be winners and they want to be seen as winners. So we need to help all our partners look good – in the eyes of their customers, their partners, their bosses, their colleagues as well as in the public eye. We need to help them to publicize their success.

 'After the game is before the game', a soccer expert once said.
So, **after the sale is before the sale.**
Let's put that into practice.

OVER TO YOU

- Give one good example and one bad example of complaint management which you have experienced.
- When you make a complaint, what kind of response do you expect? How is it different from the response you actually get? Give some examples.
- Discuss several ways in which companies can improve their after-sales service.

Test yourself!

See how much sales and purchasing vocabulary you have learned. Use the clues to complete the crossword puzzle.

Across

8   To suggest an option which you believe to be good.

9   The amount of money that a company receives in a year from the sales of its goods.

13   An event where people who work in the same industry can meet. (2 words – 5, 4)

16   When you say you are sorry, you make an … .

17   When two parties say yes: *to reach an … .*

18   A formal offer to supply goods at a particular price.

19   When an arrangement is definite, you often get written … .

21   General terms and … .

22   The other companies in your industry which perform the same functions.

24   The company which provides you with the goods you need to do your business.

25   Asking suppliers to make bids: *… to bid.*

Down

1   A small bit of thick paper with your name, the name of your company, and your contact details. (2 words – 8, 4)

2   A reduction in the price of something.

3   To describe when the goods will arrive: *… date.*

4   This is how much you have to pay.

5   An event where goods are sold to the highest bidder.

6   To make an offer, normally in a tender scenario.

7   Those costs which are fixed, regardless of how much you sell.

8   RFP is the short form of this phrase. (3 words – 7, 3, 8)

10   What you have to pay if you do something wrong.

11   Similar to a guarantee, where the seller promises to repair or replace the product if there is a problem.

12   The basic contract under which all future dealings take place: *… contract.*

14   The amount of money you have to pay for a particular service.

15   A list of the goods you have bought which says how much you have to pay.

20   To request goods from a supplier.

23   A sales team often has to sell a certain amount of goods, that is their *sales … .*

Partner files

Your name is Kate/Kyle Gorresdal and you work at the Norwegian subsidiary of International Garments Inc. You need to talk to somebody in the purchasing department at HQ in Florence who can help you order some give-aways for a trade fair. First read your notes. Then make the call.

We need:

No decision yet on budget!

500 pens
300 pencils
- all with our company logo
- delivery in 4 months
- must fit the modern design of the stand
- the colouring should be the same as the company logo

— We need good quality pens — the ones we gave away last year were horrible!

You are Leslie Sorenson and you work for Deyhle Travel GmbH in Austria. You offer travel management solutions for small and medium-sized companies. You are at your stand at the international fair *business.org*. Talk to a potential new client and ask questions about their business and background. Inquire about their needs and specifications.

We offer travel management solutions for your company!

⇒ scheduling flights
⇒ handling visas
⇒ booking accommodation
⇒ arranging international conferences
⇒ organizing client entertainment abroad

Leslie Sorensen
Regional Sales Director Europe

Deyhle Travel GmbH | Hofgasse | 21077 Graz
Telephone: (43) 0316 68 67 39 | Fax: (43) 0316 68 67 24
www.deyhle.com | l.soerensen@deyhle.com

You are Petra/Peter Nolte of Bread Basket, a large-scale bakery located in your country. You are going to phone Marie/Mario Stoll, a purchaser at Clever Catering, to make an offer. You know they offer catering and event management, and you would like to create a contact and hopefully sell them your new products. Here are some notes you have written:

What we sell: bread, rolls and biscuits

Our strengths
- We have a range of production facilities worldwide.
- We also have our own delivery services.
- Our products are always of high quality.
- We produce locally, thus the products are much fresher.

Our objectives
- Sell new products, e.g. bread and biscuits.
- Provide other specific products, e.g. for people with diabetes.
- Possible trial period either in the US or in the Middle East.

Your name is Paula/Paul and you are a purchaser in Hanse Business Bank. You have requested an offer for New Year's cards from Print Unlimited. A branch manager had recommended this supplier, but you think the offer is very expensive. Also, you have dealt with this company before (they printed business cards for you) and you are not sure how reliable their deliveries are. Look at the terms of the offer and your notes, and ring the supplier.

New Year's cards – offer from Print Unlimited

- 10,000 cards per annum *— need 6,000 cards only*
- five-year contract *— only prepared to sign two-year contract, then perhaps extend*
- a selection of three designs to choose from each year *— can we have 4 or 5 designs?*
- delivery to central headquarters by 1 December *— OK, but would prefer delivery to six regional branches, not just HQ*
- 2,500 high-quality cards *— need 1,000 only, with envelopes*
- initial price offer: €1.50 per standard card and €3.00 per premium card. *— price too high: max price is €1.00 standard, €2.00 premium (€2.50 with envelopes)*

Important: *Require penalty for late delivery (2% reduction in price?)*

UNIT 5, EXERCISE 4   **FILE 05**

You are Joseph/Josephine Peters, a buyer at the Fifth Season Hotel in Manchester. Yours is a first class hotel and you are looking for furniture for the six suites that are reserved for VIPs. You need top-quality furniture that reflects your hotel's minimalist and functional design.

You want to place the following order under a frame contract with Martha/Martin Beston at Executive Furniture Inc. in Brussels.

Use the notes below to make a phone call.

Furniture needed   (for each of six suites)

sofa/armchair	*Tuscan yellow*	1/4
coffee table		1
desk/chair		1/1
dining table/chairs		1/6
sideboard		1
double bed		1
bedside tables		2
wardrobes		2

Wood – Ahorn maple? (MA250R)

Note: goods receiving is closed 12–2 p.m. Gerald Smith will sign for goods. Mobile 0176-245 07 33
Delivery date: middle of next month, not later!!

UNIT 5, EXERCISE 11   **FILE 06**

First look at the information below and add two of your own figures to lines 4 and 5. Then call your partner and take turns passing on the information you have.
Note: Try to talk about the figures in full sentences (i.e. don't just dictate the numbers) and use language for checking and confirming information.

Tell your partner:	
1	rise in transport costs of about $350,000 (US)
2	increase in prices for raw materials 9.6% (during the last quarter of the year)
3	delivery problems with article no. HJP50-TT15
4	
5	
Take notes:	
6	
7	
8	
9	
10	

UNIT 6, EXERCISE 14   **FILE 07**

You work in the purchasing department of Illuminate Inc., a British company which produces lamps. You have received an email from your boss informing you about problems with one of your suppliers, a company in Madrid that supplies all types of promotional material. Read the email below from your boss, then ring the supplier to discuss the problems.

I saw the email from Cards 'n More where they just confirmed the shipment 'as agreed'. We don't have written confirmation of the date! Please note this for next time.

Now the pens have arrived – in the wrong colour. They also have our old company logo, not the new one. This is the second time that we've had problems with this supplier. Last time the product (name tags) was right, but we got the shipment a week late, almost too late for the conference where we needed them! And they sent a bill for additional charges.

Call them and get them to fix the problem. Also, insist on a ten per cent reduction on the total price – for both shipments!

After the conversation, you should receive an email confirming what was agreed. Make sure that everything is correct, and respond by email.

Partner files

Your name is Maria/Marco Arcoletti, senior purchaser in the central purchasing department of International Garments Inc., located at the company headquarters in Florence. You are about to receive a call from Kate/Kyle Gorresdal (one of the Norwegian sales representatives). Take the call and find out what she/he wants.

International Garments Inc. ·····················

To: (Branch Name or Department)
Global Purchasing Department   From: _____
Area 4.5 Marketing Articles   Team: _____
Headquarters, Group No. P 4.5   Branch No.: NOR 25/01

                       Internal Telephone no.:
                       _____
                       Date: _____

Requisition

1. Description and business case

Your name is Pat Thacker and you work in the Purchasing Department of Aircraft Maintenance Inc., Liverpool. Your company's sales representatives travel internationally and you are opening a new production site in Shanghai later this year. You want to outsource travel management, and are visiting the stand of Deyhle (an Austrian-based company) at the international fair *business.org*. Do they have the experience in the regions you are looking at? Are they able to handle your worldwide business from Austria?

Aircraft Maintenance Inc.

Pat Thacker
PURCHASING DIRECTOR
12 Manor Square | Liverpool LI4 6GT
Telephone: +44 (40) 53 90 98 10
Fax: +44 (40) 53 90 98 11
www.am-liverpool.com
p.thacker@am-liverpool.com

You are Marie/Mario Stoll, chief purchaser for Clever Catering in Denmark, a company which offers catering and event management in Europe. You are now branching out into the Middle East and are looking for new suppliers to satisfy the demands of your customers. You are going to receive a phone call from one of your suppliers, Petra/Peter Nolte at Bread Basket, a large-scale bakery which supplies high-quality products. Look at the notes you have written and take the call.

Objectives

- We are looking for a supplier of bread and cookies for our canteens. We need a broad range of dietary specifications: diabetes patients in some of the hospitals we deliver to.

- Requirements: consistent quality level; 17,000 rolls in the first year and about 15,000 biscuits in the first year. Guaranteed right of return for unused bread, rolls or cookies.

- Possibility: test products first on the European market?

You are a sales rep at Print Unlimited. You have already done business with Hanse Business Bank (they ordered business cards from a colleague of yours) but that was a few months ago. As you are also their client (you have all your accounts with them), your branch advisor has passed your name on to the purchasing department. They are looking for a new supplier of New Year's cards. Look at these points from your offer and the comments you've added, and take the phone call.

Offer for Hanse Business Bank

- 10,000 cards per annum
- five-year contract   — standard
- a selection of three designs to
  choose from each year   — standard
- delivery to central headquarters by 1 December
- 2,500 high-quality cards
- (initial price offer) €1.50   — can go down a
  per standard card and   bit: 1.30 standard,
  €3.00 per premium card.   2.50 premium (without
  envelopes), 2.70 (with envelopes)

Need to mention that we use recycled paper only
(due to contracts with own suppliers)

UNIT 5, EXERCISE 4   FILE 05

You are Martha/Martin Beston and work in the sales
department at Executive Furniture Inc. in Brussels.
A client is going to call you, and place an order for
hotel furniture. Take down the information. Look at
your notes below before taking the call.

Specifications (colour and quality
of upholstery, type of wood, style?)
Contact person? Will he or she be
there to sign for the goods?
Important: need signed order
before order goes to factory!!

UNIT 5, EXERCISE 11   FILE 06

First look at the information below and add two of
your own figures to lines 9 and 10. Then call your
partner and take turns passing on the information
you have.
Note: Try to talk about the figures in full sentences
(i.e. do not just dictate the numbers) and use
language for checking and confirming information.

Take notes:	
1	
2	
3	
4	
5	

Tell your partner:	
6	decrease in production: 12.6% (over last year)
7	question about order no. ATE669/13YG
8	Total price for order: €3,562.52 (including VAT)
9	
10	

UNIT 6, EXERCISE 14   FILE 07

You work in the sales department of Cards 'n More,
a large supplier of promotional material located in
Madrid. This is only your fourth week on the job
and your company seems to be going through a
crisis. You have received a number of emails and
phone messages – both from production and from
one of your customers, a British company called
Illuminate Inc. Read through the messages below.
Then get ready to answer the phone when
somebody from Illuminate Inc. calls to complain
about a problem.

From: Melina Meriopolos (Production)
To: All sales reps
Re: Recent mix-ups

Dear colleagues in sales

I am sorry to inform you that we have recently had quite a few
problems fulfilling orders correctly. This was due to our new online
ordering system, which was installed last week. It took a while to
get it running correctly, but I am happy to say that everything is now
working fine so we should have no more problems in this area.

Please note that we are currently in a rather difficult situation with
regard to the seasonal rush of orders. As you know, this is the time
of the year when we have to process the most orders, and we are
having trouble meeting the demand.
Please make sure that:
a) clients understand this situation and
b) you do not agree to any delivery time under four weeks.

Yours
Melina

Note from controlling:
Illuminate Inc. still has
not paid their bill for
the 200 watches with
their new company logo
they ordered last
month.

After the call, write an email confirming the solutions
you have agreed.

Answer key

UNIT 1

page 5

1 Carol works in sales, Dong-Sun in purchasing.

page 6

Carol: 1, 2, 4–11
Dong-Sun: 2, 3, 5, 6, 8–10, 12

2 1 d to fill in order forms
 2 c market research
 3 f to draw up tenders
 4 a to negotiate contracts
 5 e delivery date
 6 b to handle complaints

page 7

3 key account manager 3
 sales representative 1
 senior purchaser 4
 supply chain manager 2

4 1 f 5 c
 2 g 6 e
 3 b 7 d
 4 h 8 a

page 8

6 They discuss: 2.1, 2.2 and 2.4.

page 9

1 sales targets
2 increase the sales volume
3 specific goals
4 ahead of
5 improving sales
6 sales promotion
7 look into; exceed our budget
8 corporate clients

7 1 are ... on 5 exceed/be above
 2 were ... below 6 reach
 3 have ... set 7 are ... above
 4 revise

page 10

8 1 sales volume 5 sales meeting
 2 sales force 6 sales figures
 3 sales tax 7 sales promotion
 4 sales targets 8 salesperson

9 (suggested answers)
 1 Company credit cards for all flight personnel
 2 John Murphy

page 11

1 Correct.
2 Correct.
3 Incorrect. There are suppliers but Dong-Sun wants to offer a better service than just fulfilling John's specific order.
4 Correct.
5 Incorrect. Dong-Sun will assess and compare the offers.
6 Incorrect. John does not complain.

10 1 agreement 6 purchase
 2 assessment 7 request
 3 to compare 8 to solve
 4 competition 9 specification
 5 complaint 10 supplier

11 1 comparing 5 assess
 2 competition 6 requests
 3 suppliers 7 solution
 4 specifications

UNIT 2

page 13

Starter (suggested answers)
 P: a, d, i
 S: f, g, h
 P+S: b, c, e, j

1 1 False 2 True 3 True

page 14

2 1 And I'm Brigitte. *Brigitte Dupont*. Pleased to meet you.
 2 *Well, I found it very* interesting. ... *yours was definitely* one of the more relevant for me.
 3 *Can I ask* which company you are with?
 4 *I'm* a senior purchaser at Air South, responsible for engine parts.
 5 *Do you think that our MRO services* may be of interest to you?
 6 *Well, if you have time next week,* perhaps you'd be interested in meeting after the trade fair is over.
 7 Could you give me *your card*?
 8 *In the meantime,* would you like to look at our new catalogue?

3 (suggested answers)
 1 Could you tell me your name, please?
 2 Can I ask what business you are in?
 3 Would you be interested in meeting next week?
 4 Could you just wait a minute while I get my diary?
 5 Could you give me your business card/contact information?
 6 Don't you work at HT Electronics?
 7 Would you like to meet later to discuss the details?
 8 Would you like to put your name on our mailing list?

page 15

4
1 c	4 b
2 e	5 f
3 a	6 d

page 16

6 They talk about:
Brussels, sports, work, intercultural differences, beer.

1 a	4 a
2 b	5 a
3 b	6 b

page 17

7
1 What do you think of the trade fair so far?
2 Have you ever been to Wimbledon?
3 Are you planning to stay the whole week?
4 How is the weather in Chicago at the moment?
5 Do you think fairs are different in other countries?
6 Have you had a chance to look around Brussels?

1 d	D	4 c	A
2 b	E	5 f	C
3 a	B/D	6 e	F

page 18

11
1 pleasure	5 like
2 appreciated	6 suggest
3 additional	7 arrange
4 attached	8 Kind

page 19

12
1 g	5 a
2 c	6 f
3 b	7 e
4 d	

page 20

13
1 It was good to meet you and I also enjoyed your visit at our stand.
2 Thank you very much for the invitation and the opportunity to meet.
3 We would like to hear more about …
4 Could you provide some information as to the following …
5 Would 3 April at 11 a.m. in our offices be convenient?
6 I would like to confirm the meeting …
7 I look forward to seeing you in Bremen.
8 Thank you for your help. Looking forward to seeing you on 3 April.

UNIT 3

page 23

1
1 c	5 f
2 g	6 b
3 e	7 a
4 d	

2
a Marco is trying to sell their new variety of sparkling red wine, Rosso frizzante.
b Ines says that she would be happy to meet Marco, and also tells him about the invitations to tender.
c Marco will send her some bottles of the new wine.

page 24

1 are promoting; might be interested
2 in finding out
3 are convinced; international recognition
4 in your new brochure; on your website
5 may be of interest
6 in a position to offer
7 you'll be impressed

3
1 c		4 b	
2 d		5 e	
3 f		6 a	

1 special rates
2 to promote our new product
3 high-quality
4 be of interest
5 to place an order
6 put out a tender

page 25

4 (suggested answer)
Yes, Marco followed the AIDA approach with the following statements:
A: Well, this month we are promoting some of our products in Europe …
I: … did you hear that that we won an international award in Rome last month?
D: … we are always looking for new high-quality wines.
A: Just let me have our experts look at the Rosso frizzante first …

5
1 S		6 P	
2 P		7 P	
3 S		8 S	
4 S		9 P	
5 S		10 S	

a 3, 5		c 2, 9	
b 1, 4, 8		d 6, 7, 10	

page 27

7
1 Service	5 Delivery
2 Bidding	6 Warranty
3 Specification	7 Shipping
4 Budget	

page 28

8
1 g	5 d
2 e	6 b
3 f	7 c
4 a	

9
1 d
2 g
3 f
4 c
5 e
6 a
7 b

page 29

1 participate
2 fulfil
3 recommend
4 assure
5 trust
6 prevent
7 require

10 (suggested answers)
2 Product availability must be ten years (not five years).
3 We want clear bottles (not green).
4 We want medium-dry prosecco (not dry).

page 30

11 They discuss the colour of the bottles, the price and the availability.

1 Do you mean
2 Yes, I see your point.
3 if I understand you correctly
4 That's correct
5 Could you be more specific?
6 Right.
7 So, you'll get back to me
8 I see.
9 right

UNIT 4

page 32

Starter (suggested answers)
i Be honest and trustworthy.
j Look for weaknesses in your opponent's arguments.

page 33

1 (suggested answer)
b They are negotiating specific parts of the offer.

2 price
3 additional
4 five
5 5
6 costs
7 limit

2 1 duration
2 fee
3 interim
4 discount
5 terms and conditions
6 calculation

page 34

a duration
b discounts
c calculations
d terms and conditions
e fees
f interim

3 a speaker 3 b speaker 2, 4 c speaker 1, 5

page 35

4 1 leased; would receive
2 increased; could lower
3 agree; will need
4 agreed; would be able to
5 buy; receive
6 extended; would *you* reduce
7 is; will send

page 36

6 a False: she has no problem with the price. Her main objection is the long leasing period.

b False. Rachel is willing to reduce the leasing period but would have to ask more for the property. There does not seem to be much competition for the property at the moment.
c True.

1 in the ballpark
2 enables us; best interests
3 understand
4 could accept
5 may have a point
6 not with you
7 beneficial; acceptable
8 may be a possibility

page 37

7 1 receiving
2 offered
3 differ
4 suggested
5 accept
6 enable
7 reduce

8 c ✗
d ✓
e ✗
f ✗
g ✓
h ✓
i ✗
j ✗

page 38

(suggested answers)
2 b: I share your views completely. / h: I agree.
3 j: Unfortunately I can't agree with you there. / a: I see it a little differently. / f: I really can't agree with that.
4 g: Yes, I'm absolutely in favour of that option.
5 e: Up to a point we could accept that / i: Normally we could accept that

9 1 a
2 b
3 b
4 a
Yes, they've managed to reach agreement. (See email on page 39 for a summary of the conditions.)

page 39

10 Yes, everything was mentioned.
1 appreciated
2 reach
3 summarize
4 fee
5 down payment
6 confirm
7 opportunity
8 continuing

page 40

12 The following words do not fit:
2 reduce
3 lower
4 calculate
5 extend
6 a contract
7 a relationship

13 1 increase
2 discussion
3 benefit
4 difference
5 summary
6 proposal
7 calculation
8 signature
9 reduction
10 extension

UNIT 5

page 42

1
1 Tokyo
2 400
3 XPQ12
4 Osaka
5 model
6 frame
7 13,000
8 two

page 43

2 Call 1
1 would like to order
2 manage delivery
3 just make sure
4 I'll fax you

Call 2
5 ready to place
6 write this down
7 straight away
8 'll be in touch

3
1 frame contract; place of delivery
2 shipment; invoice; delivery
3 specifications
4 method of payment
5 signed order

page 44/45

5
1 b
2 f
3 d
4 g
5 c
6 a
7 e

page 46

6 Across
2 currency
5 delivery note
7 contact

Down
1 payment terms
2 confirmation
3 warehouse
4 VAT
6 value

7
1 True.
2 True.
3 False. Anna wants to make three changes (two corrections and one addition).

8 All except 2 and 6 are in the dialogue.

a: 1, 3, 7, 8
b: 2, 4, 5, 6

page 47

9 (suggested answers)
1 I'll enter the changes into the system
2 could you please tell me the order number?
3 I need to change the order.
4 I'll need written confirmation as well.
5 Could you tell me which items are incorrect?
6 Could I also ask you to add another item to the order?

10
1 82\55WR60
2 a total of 136,587; 13% (or per cent)
3 £18,500
4 850,000; 1.9 million
5 item number (or item no.) 17YTE-38R; 3.8 mm
6 €128,876.78; 19%; €153,363.37

page 48

12
1 e
2 h
3 f
4 c
5 a
6 d
7 g
8 b

1 subject matter of the contract
2 binding agreement
3 reserves all rights
4 liable for any damages
5 due date
6 interest on arrears
7 invalidate any other clauses and regulations
8 revoke this contract

page 49

13 (model answers)
1 They need to pay within fourteen days of receiving the articles. If they pay late, they have to pay four per cent interest.
2 The contract is not invalid if one clause is deleted.
3 We can select a third party to deliver the goods but, in this case, the third party is responsible for any damages.
4 We can get out of the contract if Phone Europe breaks any of the clauses.

UNIT 6

page 50

1 Call 1
Problem: They ordered ten sensors of one model, but got twenty of another.
Response: The supplier will deliver the correct sensors by Friday.

Call 2
Problem: Computer network is not working.
Response: Production will send a technician by noon.

page 51

1
1 c
2 a
3 f
4 h
5 b
6 e
7 g
8 d

2 Yes, the speakers follow the three-step approach when making their complaints.

3
1 I'm afraid that there's a problem with the invoice.
2 I'm afraid this delay will cause us problems.
3 We haven't received the shipment yet.
4 The shipment should have been sent to Moscow.
5 Unfortunately the program is still not working.
6 I can understand that this is frustrating for you.
7 Can you confirm that someone will be here tomorrow?
8 Your technicians should have fixed it yesterday.
9 Unfortunately there seems to be a mistake with the order.

page 52

4 Problem: Wrong paper shipped (wrong watermark and colour)
Solution: Correct paper will be sent by special delivery the next day

5 1 understand your situation
2 a priority for you
3 May I just ask
4 exactly do you mean
5 'll speak directly
6 'll make sure
7 personally

a 1, 2
b 3, 4
c 5
d 6, 7

page 53

6 (suggested answers)
2 I realize that must be difficult.
3 What exactly is the problem?
4 Would that be/Is that convenient for you?
5 I'll make sure you get it next week.
6 I will personally sort it out immediately.
7 I'll get back to you on Friday about the discount.

7 2 'll make sure
3 'll deliver
4 'll fax
5 'll confirm
6 'll receive

page 54

9 1 False. There is a frame contract: *LIGFC 25230 of 10 February 2009*.
2 True.
3 False. The delivery date was not confirmed.
4 True.
5 False. Linda asks for compensation, but Ineke de Bruin has not yet responded.

10 a description
b compensation
c confirmation
d information
e delivery
f shipment

page 55

1 information
2 shipped
3 confirm
4 describe
5 deliver
6 compensation

11 1 Please accept my apologies ...
2 I very much regret the frustration and problems this has caused you.
3 The delay was caused by ...
4 The missing items will be delivered by special courier ...
5 I would like to offer you ...
6 Again I regret the inconvenience ...

page 56

12 1 regret
2 comply; forced
3 assured
4 forced
5 formally
6 directly

13 (suggested answers)
Email 1
Please accept my apologies for the incorrect delivery. I realize that this must be very frustrating for you. Please be assured that we are doing everything we can do here to fix this problem, so that this situation will not happen again.
We will of course cover the extra costs. As a sign of our goodwill, we would also like to offer you a ten per cent discount on your next order.
Once again, I regret the inconvenience we have caused. If you have any further requests, please speak to me directly, and I will personally handle the situation.

Email 2
Please accept my apologies for the recent late payments. We have meanwhile installed a new system to handle invoices, so I can assure you that this kind of delay will not happen again. Regarding your messages, there must have been a mix-up, which I will sort out here.
I will personally make sure that the invoice plus charges is paid before the end of this week.

pages 58/59

Test yourself!

Across
8 recommend
9 turnover
13 trade fair
16 apology
17 agreement
18 tender
19 confirmation
21 conditions
22 competitors
24 supplier
25 invitation

Down
1 business card
2 discount
3 delivery
4 price
5 auction
6 bid
7 overheads
8 request for proposal
10 penalty
11 warranty
12 frame
14 fee
15 invoice
20 order
23 target

Transcripts

Carol
2 Well, first of all, I am constantly telephoning people and writing emails. You have to maintain contact with your clients if you want to succeed. This means that I also often visit them to present our products or to make offers. I go to a lot of trade fairs too, both to look for new contacts and to keep in touch with old clients. One thing I find quite difficult is negotiating contracts, you know, agreeing the terms and conditions of the sale. That can sometimes be tricky. And of course handling complaints is not my favourite task either, although I try to see complaints as an opportunity to improve my relationship with the customer.

In the office I spend a lot of time doing market research – the tools we have nowadays are excellent – and also looking at tenders that we may want to make a bid for. I also need to liaise with various internal departments, especially R & D and our production department. Close contact with them is important for making sure our company delivers the service that our customers are looking for.

Dong-Sun
3 A lot of my work involves writing and checking written information. We have to fill in order forms, deal with the correspondence and invoices we get, and check the details, like delivery dates and so on. I spend a lot of time collecting and comparing offers from suppliers, which means quite a lot of analysis work. And of course I have to write lots of emails – most of these are in English – and also draw up tenders and invitations to bid. Doing market research also means we have to write lots of reports for other departments in our company.

But the job isn't only a lot of paperwork; I also get out to meet people. I enjoy visiting trade fairs, for example, as it is a chance to look at the new products on the market and meet with the suppliers directly. I am also often involved in negotiations with our suppliers. For this we need to liaise closely with the business unit which has placed the order. Our department is basically responsible for making sure that our colleagues have everything they need to do their jobs.

Carol So, what about the sales meeting last week?
3 How did it go?
James It was very good, actually. They're still working on the minutes but Iris asked me to fill you in on the main points.
Carol Good.
James Well, first of all, Chin-Sun has revised our sales targets.
Carol Oh, really? So how do they look now?

James Well, the targets are quite challenging, actually. She wants to increase the sales volume by ten per cent overall. I think she's under pressure from management.
Carol Yes, maybe you're right.
James There are also some specific goals for the various regions. For example, there are going to be two new facilities: one in Dubai and one in Beijing. Apparently, we are planning to make a big push in these areas, and management thinks the time is right.
Carol Maybe it's the right attitude to have at the moment. It would be nice to really enhance our image internationally. It certainly means we'll be ahead of our new targets, if it all works out, that is.
James So, what else? India is going extremely well and most of the other areas are only just below target. The only problem is, as you know, our South American business.
Carol Right. Did Chin-Sun present my ideas for improving sales there?
James Yes, she did. Headquarters agreed that we should offer more scheduled flights and also start selling charter flights for some clients. It won't be easy to turn the situation around, apparently, but it is possible.
Carol We will also need a sales promotion specifically for the region, perhaps something like an early booking discount. I'll look into that, although I'm afraid it might exceed our budget.
James Maybe, but you're right, we should look into it. We definitely need to pull in more orders overall.
Carol OK. I could also contact the corporate clients in my area and present our new offers to them. That way we'll bring in new orders, I'm sure.
James Good idea. I'll do the same. Oh, look at the time. I'm sorry but I've got to run. Perhaps we can talk more later.
Carol OK, no problem. Thanks a lot, James. See you later.
James Bye.

John Interflights. Hello.
5 **Dong-Sun** Hello. It's Kim Dong-Sun from purchasing here. Could I speak to John Murphy, please?
John Speaking. Hi, Dong-Sun.
Dong-Sun Ah, good morning, John. Do you have a moment to talk about your request for company credit cards?
John Ah, yes. Right. Thanks for getting back to me.
Dong-Sun No problem. So, I understand you want all flight personnel to be able to draw cash in foreign locations.

John	Yes, that's right. Is there a problem? I typed all the specifications into the system yesterday. Are there no suppliers for that kind of service?
Dong-Sun	No, that's not it. As you know we have some new policies here. We want to offer a better service than just fulfilling your specific order. It is our goal to solve your problems by what we purchase. So could you help me understand the reason for the order? I understand the crews need to stay overnight a lot and in some places they need some cash.
John	That's right. Our people fly to different places around the world. Sometimes they might also have a stop-over where they need cash for a drink or a paper or even local transportation.
Dong-Sun	OK, in that case there could be a number of solutions. We could provide them with special debit cards. Or we could give our partner hotels the facility to pay a limited amount of cash to our crew and then claim this back from us.
John	Interesting. I must admit I hadn't thought of that option.
Dong-Sun	OK, what I'll do then is contact a couple of possible suppliers and arrange to get some offers. We can then compare them to see which gives us the best solution. Also, I can talk to different kinds of suppliers – not just for the credit card solution – thereby increasing the competition. It should mean we can find an even cheaper solution.
John	Sounds good. Is there anything you need from me?
Dong-Sun	Not at the moment. Thanks for your time. Bye, John.
John	Right, talk to you later, then.

UNIT 1, EXERCISE 11

6 So I wanted to update you all on the situation with the various offers purchasing has received for credit cards for the international flight crew. Dong-Sun's team is currently comparing these offers. The competition is very tough at the moment, which is of course good for us. Not all suppliers were able to meet our specifications, so they were able to exclude some offers straight away. They will have to assess the rest very carefully and perhaps put in some requests for more information. But the people in our purchasing department are very thorough, and I'm sure they will find the best solution for us.

UNIT 2, EXERCISE 1

Brigitte	Hello, uh, Mr Adams. Do you have a minute?
Donald	Yes, certainly. But please call me Donald.
Brigitte	And I'm Brigitte. Brigitte Dupont. Pleased to meet you.
Donald	Pleased to meet you too, Brigitte. So, how did you like the presentation?
Brigitte	Well, I found it very interesting. I've listened to many presentations this week, as you can imagine, and yours was definitely one of the more relevant for me.
Donald	That's good to hear. I tried to give a good overview of our range of products. Can I ask which company you are with?
Brigitte	Of course. I'm a senior purchaser at Air South, responsible for engine parts.
Donald	Air South, right. That's very interesting. Do you think that our MRO services may be of interest to you?
Brigitte	Well, that's why I wanted to talk to you. We're actually looking for new partners at the moment. I would need more details about what you can offer, of course.
Donald	Yes, I can understand that. This is perhaps not the best place to discuss details, though. Doesn't Air South have an office here in Brussels?
Brigitte	Yes, that's right. I'm actually based here in Brussels, although I'm quite often on the road.
Donald	I see. Well, if you have time next week, perhaps you'd be interested in meeting after the trade fair is over. I'd really like to hear more about your company and could give you a more detailed presentation of what we offer.
Brigitte	Yes, that's a good idea. Next week would work well. Then some of my colleagues could be there too.
Donald	Right. Could you give me your card? Then I can ring you on Friday to set up an appointment for next week.
Brigitte	Good. And meanwhile I'll speak to my colleagues and see what time is best for us. So, here you are.
Donald	And here's mine. Great, Brigitte, I'll ring you as soon as the fair is over.
Brigitte	Good, I'm looking forward to hearing from you.
Donald	In the meantime, would you like to look at our new catalogue? It has short descriptions of all the new products we're launching.
Brigitte	Thanks. I've already taken one. It was nice to meet you, Donald. Goodbye.
Donald	Good bye, Brigitte. Talk to you soon.

UNIT 2, EXERCISE 6

Brendan	Sorry, is this seat taken?
Rainer	No, no. Please, feel free.
Brendan	Thanks.
Rainer	Nice pub, isn't it? It reminds me very much of England.
Brendan	Yes, me too. Is that where you're from?
Rainer	No, I'm from Germany, but I often go to England on business.
Brendan	Really? I'm actually from Liverpool, and this sort of pub makes me feel right at home.
Rainer	Yes, I can imagine. Have you had a chance to look around Brussels while you've been here?
Brendan	Well, yes, a little. I think it's a nice place to have a fair, don't you?
Rainer	Yes, I like coming here a lot. There are quite a few of these comfortable pubs with very good beer and live football matches on TV. Um … are you interested in football?
Brendan	Yes, I am actually. Liverpool's my team.

Rainer	That makes sense. And Werder Bremen's mine. Bremen's my hometown.
Brendan	Of course. By the way, I'm Brendan – Brendan Johnson. I'm with Aircraft Maintenance Inc., in Liverpool.
Rainer	That's a coincidence. I'm also in the airline industry. Rainer Noack's my name. I'm a buyer at Low Cost Flights International in Bremen.
Brendan	Nice to meet you. So, how's your fair so far?
Rainer	Good. I've been trying to find new suppliers for special overhauls so I've been quite busy.
Brendan	I know what you mean. You know, there certainly are a lot of German companies here. It always amazes me how much in-depth information German business people provide at these fairs. They always seem to get right down to business.
Rainer	True. We Germans want to deliver solid data, with lots of facts and specifications. We don't want to waste time on a lot of unessential talk.
Brendan	That's interesting. For me the 'unessential talk' is often the most interesting. I see trade fairs as a place to get to know people, to make contacts, and not just to discuss the specifications of a particular product. You can always talk about details and the nitty-gritty later.
Rainer	Yes, I see your point.
Brendan	So, you're looking for suppliers. May I ask if you already have some information about my company?
Rainer	No, I don't think I do.
Brendan	You know, you might be interested in our brochure. Will you be staying at the fair long?
Rainer	Yes, till Friday.
Brendan	Good. Perhaps I could come by your stand some time and I could brief you on our products. I think we could have what you're looking for.
Rainer	That sounds fine. How about tomorrow afternoon?
Brendan	That sounds great.
Rainer	Here's my business card, and I'll just write down our stand number. At around 3 p.m., say?
Brendan	That sounds good. Now, tell me, what's your favourite Belgian beer? …

UNIT 3, EXERCISE 2

9

Ines	Clever Catering, Purchasing Department. Ines Stoll speaking.
Marco	Good morning, Ines. It's Marco Falcone of Vino Rubinetto here. Do you have a moment?
Ines	Yes, of course, Marco. It's nice to hear from you. How have you been?
Marco	Fine, but busy. You know how it is.
Ines	Yes, sometimes it all seems to come at once. Anyway, what can I do for you?
Marco	Well, this month we are promoting some of our new products in Europe, and we thought Clever Catering might be interested.
Ines	Yes, of course. We're always interested in finding out what's new.

Marco	But, first of all, did you hear that we won an international award in Rome last month?
Ines	Yes, I did, actually. Congratulations.
Marco	Thank you. We were very pleased. I mean, we are convinced of the quality of our products, of course, but it's quite nice to receive international recognition. The award we won was for our new variety of sparkling red wine, Rosso frizzante. Have you heard of it?
Ines	Yes, I saw it mentioned in your new brochure and I read something on your website.
Marco	Great. It's an exciting product, isn't it? Do you think this wine may be of interest to you and your clients?
Ines	Well, as you know, Marco, we are always looking for new high-quality wines. But I'm not sure we're really looking for this type of wine. It may be a little too, let me say, exotic, for our customers.
Marco	Yes, I can understand your point. I admit it is an unusual wine, but we're very confident that people will enjoy it, and it is perfect for the forthcoming spring and summer seasons.
Ines	Hmm. You have a point. By the way, Marco, we will be putting out tenders soon for the next season, so your call is just in time.
Marco	That's great. We will definitely want to put in a bid. You know, Ines, I can tell you now that we are in a position to offer you special rates for your first order, but I would prefer to come to your office and discuss the details with you. Then I could also tell you about some of our other products.
Ines	I'd be happy to meet you, Marco. Just let me have our experts look at the Rosso frizzante first and, if we are still interested, we could meet after that.
Marco	That would be great. I will send some bottles today for them to check. Perhaps we could meet in about two weeks. Is that enough time?
Ines	It should be. I'll give you a call when we're ready.
Marco	Thanks. I look forward to hearing from you. And I'm sure you'll be impressed with this wine, Ines.
Ines	OK, Marco. Thanks for the call. Bye now.
Marco	Goodbye.

UNIT 3, EXERCISE 11

10

Ines	Marco, I'm afraid there are some differences between your offer and what we asked for in the RFP.
Marco	Do you mean clear bottles versus green?
Ines	Yes, that's one of the differences. You know, we just don't like the idea of starting with green bottles and changing to clear, as you suggested in your offer.
Marco	Yes, I see your point. Well, I have some good news on that. We've spoken to our supplier again and it seems they can deliver the clear bottles earlier than expected.
Ines	So, if I understand you correctly, you will be able to supply both wines in clear bottles as we requested.

Marco	That's correct, yes.
Ines	Well, that's good. OK. The next thing is the price.
Marco	The price? Could you be more specific?
Ines	Well, especially for the sparkling red it's quite high, and definitely not within our budget.
Marco	Well, I did give you a range of prices depending on the quantity purchased …
Ines	Right.
Marco	… and 26 euros really is a good price. Remember, it's a high-quality wine and quite unique. But I'll see what I can do.
Ines	So, you'll get back to me on that?
Marco	Yes.
Ines	Good. OK. Next there's the availability.
Marco	Excuse me, the what? I didn't catch that.
Ines	Availability. We need wines that are available for at least ten years.
Marco	I see. And in our offer we said five years, right?
Ines	That's correct.
Marco	Well, that's a bit more complicated. The problem is that …

UNIT 4, EXERCISE 1

🔊 11

Gavin	Hello Gabi. Good to see you again.
Gabi	You too, Gavin. How was your journey? You drove down from Hamburg this morning, didn't you?
Gavin	Yes, that's right. Everything was fine. The German highways really are excellent if there are no traffic jams of course.
Gabi	You're lucky you missed the rush-hour traffic – that's the worst. Can I offer you tea or coffee?
Gavin	Tea, please. … Thank you.
Gabi	And here's sugar and milk if you need it. OK, let's get started, shall we? I'd first like to summarize what's happened so far, if that's all right?
Gavin	Yes, good idea.
Gabi	Right, well, as you know, we've decided to lease a new fleet of cars for our management. You've seen our specifications, and I've received your offer.
Gavin	Yes, and what is your reaction?
Gabi	Well, in general, it seems fairly competitive, but we feel the overall price is too high. You know, we've received an alternative offer with almost the same terms and conditions, and for a very good price.
Gavin	Can I ask what they're offering?
Gabi	Well, one major point is that if we leased from them, we would receive all the types of cars that we need, without any additional fees for special cases. For example, they would not charge us extra for the four or five cars with right-hand drive that we need for Britain and Ireland.
Gavin	Right. I see. Maybe we could do something there. How about this? If you took just five more cars in that region, we could lower our offer by five per cent.
Gabi	How is that possible?
Gavin	With a higher number of cars, we could pass our tax advantage on to you.

Gabi	OK, sounds good. But if we do that, if we order five more cars, we will also need a reduction in the overhead costs for repairs and maintenance.
Gavin	What you have in our offer is already a very competitive fixed price for each repair.
Gabi	Yes, well, but I was thinking, if you gave me the annual overhauls plus the mounting of winter tyres free of charge, we could shift these costs so that they come under the budget for leasing more cars in the UK.
Gavin	Aha, if I had known of that possibility, I would have offered you our special repair insurance. You see, when you pay the monthly fee for repair insurance, we cover all costs for inspections and repairs due to wear and tear. With the additional winter package, everything would be covered.
Gabi	That sounds very good. I will obviously have to do the calculations again. There is just one last thing. If we extended the duration of the contract by another four years, would you provide us with another five per cent discount on the overall price?
Gavin	Hmm, five per cent sounds a little high. I would say four per cent is the limit there, but let me get back to you. In the meantime, I'll send you the conditions for the insurance and an interim summary of our agreements by the end of this week.
Gabi	That will be fine. I'll call you early next week, and let you know how the calculations work out.
Gavin	Good. Hopefully we'll be able to sign the contract next week. Meanwhile, Gabi, I had a question about something else …

UNIT 4, EXERCISE 3

🔊 12

1

A The product is exactly what you're looking for, isn't it?

B Yes, we're happy with the product, but the price you offered is a little high at the moment. Is there any way you could reduce the price, say with a discount?

A Well, if you bought another 10,000, we would reconsider our offer.

🔊 13

2

A We could think about the delivery dates, perhaps?

B What do you mean?

A Well, maybe we can agree to order the items in the next few weeks if you think you can come down a bit on the price.

B We will certainly reduce our price if you buy before the end of the month.

🔊 14

3

A We obviously want to create long-term relationships with our customers.

B Yes, but I'm sure you agree that we also need some benefits for the relationship to continue. Can you guarantee us cheaper prices if we continue to order from you?

A Certainly. Our clients always get discounts when they stay with us over time.

4

A We've really gone down to the lowest possible price now, I'm afraid.

B But it's still not as good as the offer in terms of the service provided. And we've already discussed the fact that the repair costs, for example, will really be very minimal.

A That is correct. Of course we're convinced of the quality as well, so I'll include repair costs in our offer if you accept the price as it is.

5

A We've been mostly happy with the product so far but, of course, we are always looking at our options. So, in this case, in order to continue ordering from you, we would need these small changes to the contract.

B But we're not sure that this will still be profitable for us if we agree to these changes.

A I'm sorry, but we really have no choice. We could only extend the contract if you agreed to all the terms.

UNIT 4, EXERCISE 6

Laura	So, as you know, I'd like to discuss some of the terms in the offer you sent.
Rachel	Yes, what is your overall impression?
Laura	Well, compared to the other offers we've received so far, it's certainly in the ball park. But, as I said, we need to discuss some of the details.
Rachel	OK, where would you like to start?
Laura	Perhaps with the leasing period. It is very long.
Rachel	Yes, I agree. That enables us to offer you a better price, which I'm sure is in your best interests, isn't it?
Laura	Normally it is, yes, but unfortunately not in this case. You see, the maximum leasing period was fixed by our board of directors.
Rachel	Ah, I understand your difficulty. However, the period we are offering is the standard term here in London. If you want to differ from that, we will have to increase the leasing rate.
Laura	Normally we could accept that, but I think we also need to consider that the building has been empty for the past three months and there seem to be no other interested parties.
Rachel	You may have a point there, but the leasing period is an extremely important factor in setting our price. Maybe we could set a dynamic rate, based on your turnover at these premises.
Laura	I'm sorry. I'm not with you. What exactly are you proposing?
Rachel	Well, we could fix a basic rate that is lower than our current offer. But then we would receive a percentage of your turnover. If the café is the success we're all hoping for, it will be beneficial to both you and us. Would that be acceptable?
Laura	That may be a possibility, but I would have to talk to my boss about it and get back to you. On the next point, ...

UNIT 4, EXERCISE 9

Gavin	The way I understand the situation at the moment is that you are generally happy with all the terms of the contract; it's just the price which remains a problem.
Gabi	That's right, Gavin. We would like to create a long-term partnership. That is certainly in our best interests. But in order to start that, we really need a lower price.
Gavin	I can understand the price issue is important for you, Gabi, and we are also looking at becoming your long-term partner here. However, both parties have to benefit for that to work. Don't you agree?
Gabi	Yes, of course. But what can you offer us in relation to the price?
Gavin	Well, we can reduce the total price by five per cent if we receive a down payment of at least a third of the annual turnover within seven days of signing the contract.
Gabi	You know, Gavin, that we expected six per cent, not just five per cent.
Gavin	Unfortunately we really can't go any further with the overall price.
Gabi	Yet you are still above the other offers, if that is your last word.
Gavin	Hmm. There is one last possibility. So far we have not talked about one-day registration. That means we would register the car formally under German law and deregister it the next day. Thus we could offer them to you as used cars at a lower price.
Gabi	Is that because you would then receive state subsidies?
Gavin	Yes, that's right. That should enable us to offer you the six per cent you need.
Gabi	Well, it sounds fine to me. I'll check it internally and get back to you, but I don't see a problem at the moment.
Gavin	All right, I guess that's it, then. All other details will have to be dealt with on the basis of our standard terms and conditions. Agreed?
Gabi	That should be fine. I'll check with our lawyers and confirm it for you as well.
Gavin	Thanks. I'm happy we've found a solution, Gabi. I'll send you an email tomorrow summarizing our agreement. Then our lawyers can draft the contract.

UNIT 5, EXERCISE 1

 Call 1

Jean	TEGID, Jean Duban speaking.
Junko	Hello, Jean. It's Junko from JapanCom in Tokyo. How are you this morning?
Jean	Oh fine, Junko, thanks. And yourself?
Junko	Not bad. At least the sun is shining today.
Jean	Yes, here too – a nice improvement. So, what can I do for you today?
Junko	We would like to order some USB adapters for our network – both the XPR14 and XPQ12 models.
Jean	OK. Let me just write this down. So, model number XPR14: how many do you need?

Junko	We need 400. And then for model XPQ12, 250. Can you manage delivery to our office in Osaka by Friday morning?
Jean	Yes, of course. That's no problem. So, let me just make sure I've got everything down right. So, that's model XPR14, 400 units, and XPQ12, 250 units, to be delivered by Friday morning to Osaka.
Junko	Yes, that's right.
Jean	Fine. I'll fax you a model contract immediately. As soon as we get that back with your signature, we can send off the shipment.
Junko	OK. That sounds fine. Thanks, Jean.
Jean	My pleasure, Junko. Bye.
Junko	Bye.

Call 2

20

Alex	Phone Europe. Alex Beck speaking.
Jean	Hello, Alex. It's Jean Duban at TEGID in Lyon. I've just received your message.
Alex	Hi, Jean. Yes, thanks for getting back to me. As I said in my message, we are ready to place our first order under the frame contract.
Jean	That's great, Alex. Let me just find a pen so I can write this down. OK, go ahead.
Alex	OK, we'd like to have 13,000 extension leads.
Jean	Sorry, Alex. Did you say 13,000 or 30,000?
Alex	Thirteen. One three.
Jean	OK, 13,000. Yes, that will be fine. Obviously we need to talk about the delivery date. If I remember correctly, we promised we would deliver that quantity within two months.
Alex	Yes, that's correct.
Jean	Good. I know our production unit is ready so I'll pass the order on to them. But you will email us the form as required, right?
Alex	Of course. I'll email it to you straight away.
Jean	That's great, Alex. I'll be in touch to let you know how things are going.
Alex	Thanks, Jean. Have a nice day.
Jean	You too, Alex. Bye.

UNIT 5, EXERCISE 7

21

Roberto	Fashion Mode. Roberto Branca speaking. How can I help you?
Anna	Hello, Roberto. Anna from Stores International in Leeds here. How are you?
Roberto	Hi, Anna. I'm fine, thanks. You too, I hope. So, I saw your first order two days ago.
Anna	Yes, that's actually why I'm calling. I need to change the order, but I'm not sure if the online tool for doing that is ready yet.
Roberto	Sorry, Anna. Unfortunately that's right. It should be available next week as soon as all the features of your client access have been installed. But it's no problem. I can type the changes into the system here.
Anna	OK, thanks. But I'll need written confirmation as well.
Roberto	Yes, of course. I'll enter the changes into the system and the software will automatically generate a confirmation email. Would that be OK?

Anna	Oh, absolutely.
Roberto	So, first, could you please tell me the order number?
Anna	Yes, it's WC0001-128jh.
Roberto	OK, one moment. Right, here it is. So, what do you need changed?
Anna	First, I have two corrections. One is the place of delivery for item number seven. It ought to be Brighton, not Birmingham.
Roberto	Brighton. OK, I've got that. And the second change?
Anna	The women's T-shirts should be light green, not light blue.
Roberto	Right. That's article number six – I've changed that to light green.
Anna	Wonderful. And finally, could I also ask you to add another item to the order?
Roberto	Certainly.
Anna	Can we have 2000 women's jeans, black ...
Roberto	Black, did you say? Not blue like those for the men?
Anna	No, no, black is correct. That's model number JM-15K. They should be delivered on 9 November to Leeds.
Roberto	OK. Is there anything else I can do for you?
Anna	No, that's all for now. Thanks, Roberto.
Roberto	My pleasure. And as I said, you should be able to do this kind of thing online by the end of next week. And if it still doesn't work then, just let me know.
Anna	Great, Roberto. I really appreciate it. Thanks again. Bye.

UNIT 5, EXERCISE 10

22

1 The order number is 82\55WR60. Have you got that?
2 The sales have been great. So far this year we've sold a total of 136,587 units. That's an increase of 13 per cent over last year.
3 Good news. We can save up to £18,500 each quarter if we switch suppliers.
4 I'm pleased to report that this facility was able to increase its output from 850,000 to 1.9 million last quarter.
5 I have a question about one of the items you ordered. It's item number 17YTE-38R, the 3.8 mm cable.
6 The net total for your latest order is €128,876.78. With the Dutch VAT of 19%, this gives you a gross total of €153,363.37.

UNIT 6, EXERCISE 1

Call 1

23

Buyer	There seems to be a mistake with the shipment.
Seller	Oh, sorry to hear that. What exactly is the problem?
Buyer	Well, we placed an order for ten sensors, model number TZ20, but instead we have received twenty TZ10 sensors. I'm afraid this delay is going to cause us problems.
Seller	Yes, I can understand. We will of course send the correct models as soon as possible.
Buyer	Sorry, but I need something more specific so I can tell our customers. Can you manage delivery by Friday? That would be our absolute deadline.

Seller	Yes, of course. I can confirm that you will receive the sensors first thing Friday morning.

Call 2

24

Customer	We called you yesterday morning about the network you installed. I'm afraid that it's still not working correctly.
Sales	Oh, that's strange. I asked our service team to send a technician to take care of it immediately. Somebody should have fixed the problem yesterday.
Customer	Well, I haven't seen any technicians, and I must say I'm getting rather annoyed. Our mail order unit still can't access the system, and it's costing us money.
Sales	I realize this must be frustrating for you. How can I best help you?
Customer	I need someone here by noon or else we will have to consider switching to a different system.
Sales	By noon? That should be no problem. I'll personally get on to the service unit immediately and make sure they take care of it.
Customer	Can you confirm that someone will be here by noon? We can't afford any more delays.
Sales	Yes, I understand. I can assure you that the technician will be on your premises before twelve o'clock.
Customer	OK, thanks.

UNIT 6, EXERCISE 4

25

Alena	Hello. Alena Novák speaking.
Linda	Hello, Alena. It's Linda Matthews at Logistics International here.
Alena	Hello Linda. How are things in Glasgow?
Linda	Well, not so good. Unfortunately, there's a problem with the latest shipment.
Alena	Oh, I'm sorry, Linda. What seems to be the problem?
Linda	We ordered your special premium paper for our copiers and printers a week ago, but we've received the wrong paper, and we have some very urgent orders coming up.
Alena	Right, I understand your situation. Of course you can't send out your material with the wrong paper.
Linda	No we can't, and our deadlines are approaching.
Alena	OK, Linda, I realize this is a priority for you so I'll see to it immediately. May I just ask you a few questions first?
Linda	Yes, sure.
Alena	What exactly do you mean by the wrong paper? I mean, is it the thickness, the size, the colour, or the quality?
Linda	Actually, the major problem is that the paper has a watermark that's not ours. Also, the paper's standard white instead of cream white as ordered.
Alena	Right, and can I just ask one more thing? I see from my documents that you also ordered shipments of standard white paper. Is that correct?
Linda	Yes, that's used for internal documents. But we ordered the other type of paper last week.

Alena	Of course. There must have been a mix-up. I'll speak directly with Production and arrange a special delivery to you by 10 a.m. tomorrow. Would that suit you?
Linda	That's fine. I think we can wait until then. Can you guarantee that delivery time?
Alena	Yes, absolutely!
Linda	We really can't afford any more problems.
Alena	I understand. I'll make sure the shipment is at your location no later than 10 a.m. tomorrow. I'll also fax you a copy of the original order. Could you please fax it back to me immediately with your signature for confirmation?
Linda	Yes, that's no problem.
Alena	Thanks, Linda. I'm really sorry about this and I'll personally make sure you get the right paper tomorrow.
Linda	Thanks, Alena. Bye.
Alena	Bye, Linda.

A–Z word list

Translation

Translation

A in **accordance with**
[ɪn ə'kɔːdəns wɪð]
to **achieve** [ə'tʃiːv]
acquainted, to get ~ with
[get ə'kweɪntɪd wɪð]
apology [ə'pɒlədʒi]
appointment [ə'pɔɪntmənt]
to **appreciate** [ə'priːʃieɪt]
approval [ə'pruːvl]
to **approve** [ə'pruːv]
assessment [ə'sesmənt]
to **assure** [ə'ʃʊə]
to **attach** [ə'tætʃ]
attention [ə'tenʃn]

B **batch** [bætʃ]
benefit ['benɪfɪt]
bid [bɪd]
board of directors
[,bɔːd əv də'rektəz]
to **build a relationship**
[,bɪld ə rɪ'leɪʃnʃɪp]

C **calculation** [,kælkju'leɪʃn]
call-off ['kɒl ɒf]
cautious, to be ~ [bi 'kɔːʃəs]
challenging ['tʃælɪndʒɪŋ]
circumstance ['sɜːkəmstəns]
to **collect** [kə'lekt]
commercial [kə'mɜːʃl]
commitment [kə'mɪtmənt]
to **compare** [kəm'peə]
compensation
[,kɒmpən'seɪʃn]
competitor [kəm'petɪtə]
concession [kən'seʃn]
condition [kən'dɪʃn]
to **confirm** [kən'fɜːm]
consistent [kən'sɪstənt]
convention [kən'venʃn]
to **convince** [kən'vɪns]
to **cooperate** [kəʊ'ɒpəreɪt]
correspondence
[,kɒrɪ'spɒndəns]
counterpart ['kaʊntəpɑːt]
customer service
[,kʌstəmə 'sɜːvɪs]

D to **deal with** ['diːl wɪð]
designed, to be ~ to
[bi dɪ'zaɪnd tə]
desire [dɪ'zaɪə]
distributor [dɪ'strɪbjətə]
to **draft** [drɑːft]
draft (version) ['drɑːft vɜːʃn]
to **draw up** [,drɔː 'ʌp]

E to **enable** [ɪ'neɪbl]
to **enhance** [ɪn'hɑːns]
to **establish** [ɪ'stæblɪʃ]
to **exclude** [ɪk'skluːd]
executive board
[ɪg'zekjətɪv bɔːd]
expertise [,ekspɜː'tiːz]
to **exploit** [ɪk'splɔɪt]
to **extend a contract**
[ɪk,stend ə 'kɒntrækt]

F **facility** [fə'sɪləti]
faulty ['fɔːlti]
to **file a tender**
[faɪl ə 'tendə]
to **fix a meeting**
[,fɪks ə 'miːtɪŋ]
fixed-price basis
[,fɪkst praɪs 'beɪsɪz]
flow [fləʊ]
frame contract
['freɪm kɒntrækt]
franchising company
[,fræntʃaɪzɪŋ 'kʌmpəni]

G to **get out of** [get 'aʊt əv]
to **get the go-ahead**
[get ðə ,gəʊ ə'hed]
goal [gəʊl]
gross [grəʊs]
guarantee [,gærən'tiː]

H to **handle a complaint**
[,hændl ə kəm'pleɪnt]
headquarters
[,hed'kwɔːtəz]

I **in-depth information**
[ɪn ,depθ ɪnfə'meɪʃn]
inconvenience
[,ɪnkən'viːniəns]
indication [,ɪndɪ'keɪʃn]
inventory ['ɪnvəntri]
invoice ['ɪnvɔɪs]
involved, to be ~ in
[bi ɪn'vɒlvd ɪn]

K **key account** [,kiː ə'kaʊnt]

L to **liaise with** [li'eɪz wɪð]
logistics [lə'dʒɪstɪks]

M to **maintain** [meɪn'teɪn]
to **make sure** [,meɪk 'ʃʊə]
to **manage** ['mænɪdʒ]
manners ['mænəz]
market research
[,mɑːkɪt rɪ'sɜːtʃ]
to **move up** [,muːv 'ʌp]

Translation

N to **negotiate** [nɪˈɡəʊʃieɪt]
to **number crunch** [ˈnʌmbə krʌntʃ]

O **objective** [əbˈdʒektɪv]
offer [ˈɒfə]
to **operate** [ˈɒpəreɪt]
overall [ˌəʊvərˈɔːl]
overhead [ˈəʊvəhed]
to **overhear** [ˌəʊvəˈhɪə]

P to **paraphrase** [ˈpærəfreɪz]
to **pass on to** [ˌpɑːs ˈɒn tə]
penalty [ˈpenlti]
performance level [pəˈfɔːməns levl]
pitch [pɪtʃ]
to **place an order** [ˌpleɪs ən ˈɔːdə]
pre-screening [priːˈskriːnɪŋ]
to **prevent** [prɪˈvent]
price tag [ˈpraɪs tæɡ]
procedure [prəˈsiːdʒə]
procurement [prəˈkjʊəmənt]
profitability [ˌprɒfɪtəˈbɪləti]
project team [ˈprɒdʒekt tiːm]
to **promote** [prəˈməʊt]
promotion [prəˈməʊʃn]
to **prompt** [prɒmpt]
provision [prəˈvɪʒn]
to **publicize** [ˈpʌblɪsaɪz]

Q **quarter** [ˈkwɔːtə]

R **ranking** [ˈræŋkɪŋ]
rapport [ræˈpɔː]
rate [reɪt]
to **reconsider** [ˌriːkənˈsɪdə]
to **refer to** [rɪˈfɜː tə]
to **reimburse** [ˌriːɪmˈbɜːs]
requirement [rɪˈkwaɪəmənt]
requisition [ˌrekwɪˈsɪʃn]
to **resolve** [rɪˈzɒlv]
responsibility [rɪˌspɒnsəˈbɪləti]
retailer [ˈriːteɪlə]
to **retain** [rɪˈteɪn]

S to **sample** [ˈsɑːmpl]
schedule [ˈʃedjuːl]
to **see to** [ˈsiː tə]
service [ˈsɜːvɪs]
to **set up a meeting** [ˌset ʌp ə ˈmiːtɪŋ]
shipment [ˈʃɪpmənt]
to **sign for** [ˈsaɪn fə]
sign of goodwill [ˌsaɪn əv ɡʊdˈwɪl]
to **source** [sɔːs]
to **submit a tender** [səbˌmɪt ə ˈtendə]
specialist [ˈspeʃəlɪst]
specification [ˌspesɪfɪˈkeɪʃn]
stock market [ˈstɒk mɑːkɪt]

Translation

strategic account [strəˌtiːdʒɪk əˈkaʊnt]
to **streamline** [ˈstriːmlaɪn]
structure [ˈstrʌktʃə]
sub-contractor [ˌsʌbkənˈtræktə]
supplier [səˈplaɪə]
supply chain [səˈplaɪ tʃeɪn]
to **switch** [swɪtʃ]

T **target** [ˈtɑːɡɪt]
to **tend to** [ˈtend tə]
tender [ˈtendə]
terms and conditions [ˌtɜːmz ənd kənˈdɪʃnz]
thorough [ˈθʌrə]
tough [tʌf]
to **track** [træk]
trial period [ˌtraɪəl ˈpɪəriəd]

V **vague** [veɪɡ]
vendor [ˈvendə]
volume [ˈvɒljuːm]

W **warranty** [ˈwɒrənti]
win-win [ˌwɪn ˈwɪn]
to **wrap it up** [ˌræp ɪt ˈʌp]

Useful phrases and vocabulary

Describing your company/department
I work in the sales/purchasing department of a small/
  medium-sized/large company called ...
We develop/make/produce/sell/...
Our department is divided into ...
We need to liaise/work closely with ...
We also are more actively involved in ...
My team/group makes sure that ...

Describing your responsibilities
My team is responsible for ...
I am in charge of ...
My main responsibility is ...
A lot of our/my work involves ...
We have to/need to ...
I spend a lot of time ...
My job also includes ...

Asking indirect questions
Can I ask which company you are with?
Doesn't your company have an office here?
Don't you work at HT Electronics?

Using would/could
Could you tell me your name (again), please?
Could you give me your business card / contact
  information?
Would you like to look at our new catalogue?
Would you be interested in meeting next week?
I could come to your office next week.

Saying who you are
This is Adam Brown from XYZ Ltd.
It's David Dietrich from purchasing here.
Hi Sarah. It's Frank here.

Getting through to the right person
Could you put me through to your purchasing
  department, please?
Could/Can I speak to John Murphy, please?
I'd like to speak to Jill, please.
I'd like to speak to somebody in your sales/purchasing
  department, please.
Is Michelle there at the moment?

Greetings and introductions
Good morning/afternoon.
Hello. My name is ...
Please call me ...
May/Can I introduce myself?
Nice/Pleased to meet you (too).

Moving on to business
How did you like the presentation?
What do you think of ...?
Have you found anything of interest?
What line of business are you in?
Let me give you/Here's my (business) card.

Arranging to follow-up
Would it be possible to arrange/fix/set up a meeting?
Could I come to see you?
Could I call you in the next few days?
Perhaps I could send you some information.
Would you be interested in meeting after the fair?
Could you send me your price lists?
I'll send you an email/give you a call next week.

Starting a conversation
Is this your first time here/in Belgium?
What do you think of Brussels/the fair?
Are you interested in football/films/winter sports?
The weather here has just been fantastic/horrible.

Keeping the conversation going
Are you interested in any particular sport?
– Yes, I'm really into snowboarding. How about you?
Have you been to Liverpool before?
– Yes, I've been there many times, actually. I really like
  the atmosphere, and the people are friendly.

Moving on to business
So, are you looking for suppliers?
Right, should we get down to business?

Salutations and closes
Dear Mr, Mrs, Ms	Regards/Sincerely
Dear Bob	Best wishes/Kind regards
Hello/Hi Bob	All the best/Best

Opening sentence

It was nice to meet you at the conference last week.
I'm writing to tell/ask you about … / Just wanted to get in touch to …
Hope you had a nice weekend.
How are things going?

Requesting information

Could you send me some details about …?
I would also like to take the opportunity to find out more about …
Would you mind answering the following questions to help us with our preparation?
We would like to hear more about …

Making or confirming an appointment

How about Thursday at 4 p.m?
Would 3 April at 11 a.m. at our offices be convenient for you?
I would like to confirm the meeting for 3 April at 11 a.m.

Concluding

Please feel free to contact me again.
I look forward to seeing you in London.
Looking forward to seeing you on 3 April.

ACTIVE LISTENING

Back-channeling – showing that you are really listening

Mmmh, good.
Yeah, OK.
Ah ah. I see.
Right.

Prompting – asking for more information

Interesting. Could you tell me more about that?
Yes, could you give me some more details?
Would you be able to provide more specific information?

Paraphrasing – making sure you have understood correctly

So you'd like …, but only if …. Is that right?
So, if I understand you correctly, you need …
Sorry, did you say …

Confirming – saying that you have understood

That's correct, yes.
That's right.
Yes, I see your point.
So, you'll get back to me on that.

AGREEING AND DISAGREEING

Agreeing

I share your views completely.
We could go along with that.
Yes, I'm absolutely in favour of that option.
I agree.

Disagreeing

I see it a little differently.
That may well be right, but …
Up to a point we could accept that, but …
I really can't agree with that.
Normally we could accept that, but in this case …
Unfortunately, I can't agree with you there.

TALKING ABOUT A PRODUCT

Asking if your partner is interested

Would you be interested in trying our …?
Perhaps I can tempt you to sample our …?
Do you think your company might be interested in …?
Do you think this may be of interest to you and your clients?

Showing interest

That sounds interesting.
That would certainly be of interest to us.
That might be exactly what we are looking for.
Could you send me a sample/give me some more information?

Being cautious

Well, maybe. But I would need to know more about …
I'm not so sure.
I don't think that's really what we're looking for.
That (really) depends on your conditions/price.

Saying you are not interested

I'm sorry but …
Unfortunately we're not looking for that at the moment.
Thanks, but we already have a supplier for that product.
No, thanks. We're not interested in that at this stage.

NEGOTIATING

Starting the conversation

We're very happy to be meeting you today.
We hope to come to an acceptable solution for both/all of us.
I'd like to discuss some of the details in the offer.
We'd like to hear your proposals before we tell you what we can offer.

Concluding your arguments

We are sure that you will see the benefits for your company if you take up our offer.
There you have our proposal. I'm afraid that's as far as we can go.
So that wraps it up.
That sums up our side then.

Finishing the conversation

That may be a possibility but I have to discuss it with my boss.
Let me get back to you.
I'm happy we've found a solution. I'll send you an email tomorrow summarizing our agreement.

HANDLING ORDERS

Placing orders
We would like to order/have …
We're ready to make our first order under the frame contract.
We'd like to place a call-off order for …
We would appreciate delivery by Friday. Can you manage it/that?

Taking orders
I'll just take/write down the details.
Let me just write this down/type in your order.
So, how many do you need exactly?
Was there anything else you'd like to order today?

Checking and confirming information
Let me just check/repeat that.
Let me make sure I've got everything down right.
Yes, that's right/correct.
Sorry, David. Did you say …?
Could you say that again/repeat that, please?

COMPLAINING

I'm afraid (that) there is a problem with …
There appears/seems to be a mistake/mix-up …
Unfortunately, we have a slight problem with …

COMPLAINT MANAGEMENT WITH CASH

Confirming you have understood the client's situation
I'm sorry to hear that. / I understand your situation.
I realize this must be frustrating for you.

Asking for the details of the problem
Could you tell me exactly which item was damaged?
May I ask if you've tried to use the tracking facility on our website?

Serving your client by suggesting solutions
You will get the missing shipment within 24 hours.
I'll get back to you first thing tomorrow morning about compensation.

Helping your client by confirming your commitments
I'll see to it immediately and personally make sure you get compensation.
Are we agreed that you'll fax me a copy of the invoice and I'll send you the missing items today?

LETTERS OF COMPLAINT AND APOLOGY

Making complaints
I'm writing to you to complain about …
I am writing in reference to the above order. Unfortunately, …

Talking about consequences
We expect you to cover these costs.
We expect compensation for the inconvenience caused.
We cannot accept this and will have to cancel our contract if it happens again.
If you do not comply with the delivery terms as agreed in our frame contract, we will be forced to contact our lawyers.

Offering apologies
Please accept my apologies for …
Please be assured that we are doing everything …
I (very much) regret the inconvenience we have caused.

Referring to future action
We will, of course, cover the extra costs/reimburse you/arrange for a new shipment …
As a sign of goodwill, I would like to offer …

USEFUL VERBS (IN CONTEXT)

		Translation
to build a relationship	It is vital to build a good relationship with those you do business with.	
to convince	I will need some more information before you can convince me to buy.	
to file/submit a tender	The closing date for filing the tender is Friday.	
to fulfil	I'm afraid your product doesn't seem to fulfil our requirements.	
to handle a complaint	It is important to handle complaints well if we want to keep our clients.	
to make sure	We must always make sure we listen to our clients' needs.	
to negotiate	I am sure we will be able to negotiate terms that are beneficial to us both/all of us.	
to place an order	I placed an order last month and it's still not arrived.	
to present	Today I want to present our latest product to you.	
to reimburse	We would like to reimburse you for the cost of replacing the faulty product.	
to set up a meeting	We should set up a meeting to discuss your product further.	